Anything is Possible

To Eric Jones

LEO DICKINSON

Anything is Possible

JONATHAN CAPE

THIRTY-TWO BEDFORD SQUARE LONDON

by the same author

Filming the Impossible

Leo skydiving

First published 1989
© Leo Dickinson 1989
Jonathan Cape Ltd, 32 Bedford Square, London WC1B 3SG

A CIP catalogue record for this book
is available from the British Library

ISBN 0-224-02826-X

Phototypeset by Computape (Pickering) Ltd, North Yorkshire
Printed in Italy by New Interlith S.p.A. – Milan

CONTENTS

1 · BALLOON OVER THE HIMALAYAS

I felt as if I could reach out and touch the mountains as we floated by.

Having taken off from the Kathmandu valley in a thick blanket of early-morning mist, the relief was exquisite now that our two balloons had plopped clear of its sodden restraint and lifted into the sunlight. We were, I felt, leaving our Mother Earth ship for the great adventure of space. The whole Himalayan chain lay stretched like a relief model around us, a model invaded by grey liquid fog that rolled down its valleys and hid its rivers from our view.

Guarisankar we could recognize clearly on our left, and Everest ahead to the north, Numbur, Kangtega ... There were landmarks enough, heads above the mist, by which to plot our course. Chris Dewhirst, navigator and expedition leader, hauled into the basket a large sheet of plywood on to which he had Sellotaped all the maps we might conceivably need, and checked our position. Then he lowered it back over the side: no problems there, we were right on track. So it gave us a wry sense of amusement when the radio crackled into life and the captain of the other balloon asked: 'Which one's Everest?' Remote and lunar as this landscape was, there could be no mistaking the highest point on earth!

The plan was to fly towards Everest, trying to get into the jetstream winds that are encountered at around 30,000 feet, and to let them carry us clear over some of the highest peaks in the world before descending to find a safe place to land, perhaps in the Dudh Kosi valley. Originally, we had wanted to overfly Everest itself, but our hard-won permits only covered Nepal and we dared not risk coming down beyond its borders. Everest's northern slopes lie squarely in Tibet – Chinese territory – and out of bounds for us.

We were three in each balloon. Chris and I occupied the green, white and yellow one with J & B emblazoned in red on its side and with Aden Wickes as pilot. For Aden, this was something of a busman's holiday: in his everyday

1   The first trans-Himalayan balloon flight leaving Kathmandu

life he is a senior jumbo-pilot for Qantas. At some time or other he has flown everything from Tiger Moths to airships, but I worried that he might now have become so accustomed to the smooth efficiency of the flight deck, that he would be tempted to abort our whimsical, unpowered passage prematurely. For all this was high and hostile terrain and we in a vulnerable craft, we did not want our flight brought to an end just as it began to get 'interesting'. Aden had already shown us how much he relished the good life by quickly disappearing at the first mention of acclimatization training. While the rest of us tramped around Everest, building up our red blood cells, Aden high-tailed it back to Kathmandu where a bit of charm and sweet-talk soon had him flying reconnaissance missions in the King's own helicopter! Aloft, my fears were subsiding. So far, he was clearly finding the trip every bit as much of a thrill as Chris and I.

The other balloon, a bright daffodil globe, was sponsored by Zanussi and had Brian Smith at the helm. Brian is a swashbuckling Yorkshireman who now lives in Australia, but wherever he is, he works hard at portraying the eccentric Victorian traveller. He has boundless energy and a head full of elaborate schemes. He only stops talking when he is asleep. And not always then. He had gone solo on his very first balloon trip, I learned, when a strong wind blew, and the instructor fell clean out of the basket on take-off. As he rose rapidly, people on the ground screamed at him to pull the rip-line, but if he was going to crash, he thought, there seemed little reason not to have a decent flight first! When eventually he decided it was time to come down, he made what he described as his best landing ever. Now he is one of the most experienced balloon pilots in Australia and runs a company specializing in the design and construction of 'inflatables'. With him in the basket were Phil Kavanagh, another Australian balloon manufacturer, and Jan Reynolds from Vermont, USA, who is best known as a mountaineer. The idea of a trans-Himalayan balloon expedition had first come to Chris and Brian in a Sydney bar and its organization had been handled mainly from Australia, although the final line-up of balloonists, film-crew and supporters turned out to be fairly international.

The producer of our film was Dick Dennison, in many ways the epitome of the movie-mogul. He had very definite ideas on what he wanted and schemed hard to get them accepted, using gentle persuasion or outright bullying, whichever he felt most appropriate to the task. He had a knack for anticipating trouble, and indeed, generally helped it along, believing implicitly in a policy of divide and rule. It was impossible to argue with this man who had spent many years as a television presenter and knew all the tricks. Nevertheless, he was a charmer, and his tactics were fun to watch, so

2 Chris Dewhirst and Aden Wickes breathing oxygen at almost the height of Everest

long as you were not the pawn in play at the time. Only the ebullient Chris Dewhirst, one-time mountaineer and now a tour-operator, ever succeeded in outwitting him, and then but rarely. Chris was another expatriate Englishman turned pure Aussie, and one who had been quick to grasp the newest technology in high-altitude, long-distance ballooning. He had tremendous enthusiasm and, once he had given himself to an idea, let nothing get in the way of realizing it. Even writing off our first balloon on its maiden flight made no dent in his incurable optimism. It was almost entirely due to him that at the end of three and a half years of frantic planning, of diplomatic missions to the governments of four nations, of financial deals wrestled from film-makers and other business magnates, here we were, rising gently in the thin, Nepalese air.

During the monsoon in August, bridges had been swept away and villages cut off by landslips. Game reserves had lost crocodiles when they were flushed down swollen rivers. And in October, when we first arrived in Nepal, it had rained and hailed and snowed for ten days without stopping. All over Nepal trekking parties were stranded in the mountains, while on Everest four Indian climbers died of exposure. Amid such chaos, clearly we were not going to be able to travel anywhere by road or trail. Our plans had been to test-fly the balloons and do some initial filming up in the Everest region

3 *above:* Acclimatizing at Gokyo (18,000 ft), Everest in the background
4 *opposite:* The *Zanussi* balloon rising above the early-morning mists over Kunde, where
   Edmund Hillary made his Sherpa Hospital. Behind is Ama Dablam.

while gradually accustoming ourselves to high altitude with easy treks. Since
we could no longer be portered in, we were obliged, once the situation eased,
to hire helicopters to take us as far as Lukla, the little airstrip south-west of
Everest. The expedition budget soared.

We suffered the usual bouts of dysentery and sickness, but by the second
week in November, back in Kathmandu once more, we felt fit and ready to
attempt the altitude flight that was to be the highlight of our expedition. It
was just a question of waiting for a suitable day. Finally our meteorologist
Martin Harris, his hotel room bristling with satellite equipment, came up
with a forecast, which though not brilliant seemed reasonably promising.
We decided to go for it.

On the Big Day we were up long before dawn, and at 4 o'clock were
spreading out the ballons in a field just outside the city by the light of truck
headlights. The unexpected appearance of thick mist was disconcerting, but

5 *above:* Mandy enthusiastically opening the mouth of the huge *J & B* balloon prior to the Everest flight
6 *opposite:* Fixing remote cameras to a line suspended from the edge of the balloon envelope

we hoped to be able to rise above it. The *J & B* balloon was inflated first and tethered to a truck to prevent it escaping while the other was filled with hot air. Using a climbing karabiner, I suspended one of my movie-cameras from *J & B*'s envelope, ready to record the flight. There was little room for us in the baskets once all our equipment and survival gear was aboard, but in we crammed and were at last ready for take off. It was only later I learned that overloading had caused us to jettison some of our fuel.

Before we had risen more than 300 feet, I looked up to see *Zanussi* directly above us, with the sharp corner of its basket thrust hard into the top of our swelling envelope. The significance of this did not strike me right away, but it soon became clear it could easily rip a giant hole in our balloon fabric and finish us off before we had properly started. With bated breath we waited, helpless, while Brian attempted to coax his two-ton monster out of our hair with a burst on his burners. Slowly he rose clear, and no damage done, but it had been a close-run thing and we were all a bit shaken. Then, at the very moment of deliverance, the eyepiece dropped from my Aaton camera and fell away to the ground. This was one filming problem I could have done without. Why is it, I wondered, that no matter how long you have to make your preparation, the last moments before you get started are always so fraught? Nor does this state of high-tension let up until the trip is over; it

continues to bombard you with unforeseen crises. Batteries mysteriously lose their charge, cameras jam, items go missing – and eyepieces fall overboard.

We were gaining height rapidly. At 10,000 feet I put on my oxygen mask but, acclimatized and fit, did not feel the need to switch it on before reaching 25,000 feet. It was not as if I was using up any energy in the bottom of the basket, but I was feeling grateful for the down clothing which had seemed so superfluous in the muggy warmth of the valley. There was plenty to do: I suspended another camera from the balloon, fixed to a hanging stick and tilted down at 45° to take in the scene of our basket with its moving back-drop. A further movie camera was attached to the burner frame, with a fish-eye lens pointing straight down upon us. Nothing was going to escape me; I had the whole basket bugged!

At about 24,000 feet we had started to feel the winds strengthen, pulling our flight path towards Everest. As we approached the higher mountains, the gap between the two balloons was widening. Aden, I could see, was enjoying every minute of his captaincy. The winds were not as strong as he would have liked: if we wanted to get right in among the Himlayan giants, there was no doubt now that we would have to pop up to 30,000 feet and get into the jetstreams proper. With two out of our three burners blazing we started the climb.

By 28,000 feet our ascent rate had fallen to 150 feet a minute, and Aden reluctantly decided to call it quits. We were not going to get up to the height of Everest, whose summit towered another 1,000 feet above us.

Suddenly, instead of the accustomed roaring in our ears, there was an uncanny silence.

Both burner lights had blown out, and we were adrift, unable to gain height or even to maintain our current level. As the seconds ticked by, consternation on the faces of Chris and Aden told me things were getting out of hand. Aden tried frantically to strike the igniters on his side, while Chris did the same on the other. In as calm a voice as he could manage, Aden called for the matches. Chris fumbled in his pockets, came out with a box – and promptly opened it upside down, scattering most of the contents to the four winds. Just one match remained, gripped between his thumb and forefinger; our lives depended on it.

By now the balloon had gone into a rapid downward spiral and the mountains were spinning past our eyes every thirty seconds. Before the emergency started I had been filming happily and, almost without thinking, now kept the camera running, thrusting it first into Aden's face, then at Chris, in an endeavour to get right in among the action. After a few minutes and a loss of several thousand feet, Aden yelled at me to put the bloody thing down, but what he said next was lost inside his oxygen mask. I decided he must be telling me to abandon ship and began tightening my parachute harness. God knows where I would have come down, but my only thought was to buy them precious time by getting out. It was only later that I learned what Aden was actually trying to get through to me: could I stop fiddling with toys and get the third burner alight? As it was, I had one leg thrown over the side of the basket when out of the corner of my eye I saw a spark of light. Chris had struck his match and our burners were blazing once more.

Aden had always said that if ever we needed to use all three burners, it would be an emergency. Well, we had all three burning furiously now! Over 10,000 feet of altitude had been lost and at 3,000 feet above the ground we were still on a relentless downward course. The renewed burst of hot air had no more effect than to slow us down a bit, like a parachute, and it was still in my mind to jump out. I stayed put, however, and we finished up bouncing around close to the valley floor, and even closer to the enveloping mountain walls. Already we were running short of fuel and it was clear we would never recover sufficiently to continue as far as we had planned. There was nothing for it but to find a place to land.

As we rushed in on the dark side of the valley, a ridge suddenly reared up in front of us. With the burners Aden managed to slow us down smoothly so that the first I knew we had touched ground was when a tree appeared over his left shoulder. Immediately, Chris jumped out with a line to try and manoeuvre us towards a snowy clearing. We watched transfixed as he began leaping like a kangaroo over 10-foot trees, clinging desperately to the rope while gravity and the balloon's natural bounce did battle.

Once more, Aden instucted me to stop filming and do something useful. I baled out and grabbed hold of the rope alongside Chris. Between us we managed to drag the monster down the slopes while the basket, with Aden still inside, crashed and banged into trees and boulders, pushing a small avalanche of snow in front of it, and coming to rest finally in a little clearing at the bottom of the hill. It took a few minutes for the good news to sink in, but we were all down safely!

We were also stranded. After brief contact with the other balloon, which we learned was also endeavouring to come down, we lost them altogether. In thick forest, a long way from anywhere, we wondered what to do next. Well, the first priority was obviously a cup of tea, only after that could we hope to

7 *overleaf:* Balloons dwarfed by the Himalayas

think things out properly! We had forgotten to bring the drinking water. If we wanted a brew, we were first going to have to melt some snow. Chris got a stove alight, but plainly it was going to be a lengthy business. I began to get irritated. Was this the best we could do?

'Aden,' I said, 'do you have any gas left in those burners?'

'Well, probably enough for another 20 minutes' flying. No more.'

'Right!'

With the billycan jammed on top of a spanner, and the spanner pushed through the burner rings, I topped up with snow, and lit up. Very soon we had two pints of boiling water. It would be no bad thing, I mused, if all expeditions were to equip themselves with a balloon burner for brewing up. It could revolutionize Himalayan climbing. Rather proud of my ingenuity, I went on to make some noodle soup. This was the point at which I overreached myself: I thought I could thicken it up with muesli, but the cereal floated on top in a soggy scum. Chris went off to look for the others.

When he stumbled back, exhausted, hours later, we learned he had managed to contact them by shouting across a ravine. Thick rhododendron scrub had prevented him getting any closer. All were safe, he said, but they had had an amazing escape. They crashlanded through trees and finished upside down under their basket with their burners on. Dry twigs all around immediately caught alight and within seconds they were engulfed in flame. Jan Reynolds had managed to wriggle free and beat out the fire before pulling the others clear. The balloon was a write-off.

A basket fire is serious at the best of times, but trapped underneath it like that, the consequences could so easily have proved fatal. It didn't bear thinking about! They had been remarkably lucky. Now, like us, they were holed up at the bottom of this valley, surrounded by near-impenetrable forest. Our combined gear lay scattered across assorted mountainsides.

Chris had come face to face with a small bear in the forest, he told us, and then a yeti. It had large floppy ears and spoke excellent English. He was too tired to elaborate on this and we remained mystified. The strain of the day had obviously taken its toll. We pitched our tent and prepared for a chilly night. There was just one thing to do before turning in: we must spread out the balloon envelope as a marker in case our helicopter should come looking for us.

That night four inches of snow fell, effectively painting out our signal, so the first job next morning was to clear it off again. A couple of hours later I spotted a light aircraft, one of the Everest sight-seeing flights, and Aden was quick to make contact with it on our VHF radio. Now, at least, someone knew where we were. In little over another hour, a helicopter could be heard droning up our valley. Aden expertly guided it in through the thick gathering cloud to an improvised helipad stamped out in the bare patch of snow where our tent had stood.

'I've brought you some more gas and oxygen, so you can continue your flight,' Dick Dennison announced, as he jumped out.

The news was greeted with considerable astonishment. Even if our abbreviated flight had failed to take us far into the Himalayas, still we had been up for two and a half hours and enjoyed magnificent views — all of which we had safely in the can. We had been able to see 70 miles into Tibet, to the lakes beyond Everest, and for our first trans-Himalayan flight believed we had done quite well. It had certainly not been lacking in excitement. None of us saw it as the failure Dick seemed to be implying, nor did we feel at all like going on. Not there and then anyway. Chris and I had discussed the possibility of another flight later, but it was clear that what Dick wanted to see was more Action, capital A, *now*. Soon he and Aden were locked in a heated argument, while the rest of us sat by helplessly.

The situation was resolved at last by the helicopter pilot, who was concerned for the safety of his machine in the worsening light and announced that he had to leave. *Right away!* He would get someone to come and pick us up as soon as possible, he said. Tomorrow, most likely. Would Mr Dennison-Sahib please climb back inside? There was nothing else for it, Mr Dennison-Sahib clambered aboard.

As far as I was concerned, the filming was finished for this flight. I had used up all my film, so I shoved the camera equipment into the helicopter with them. That would be one less thing to worry about and at least our precious film would be safe.

The following morning, true to his word, the captain returned, and this time lifted out the basket and burners. Forty minutes later he was back again to take away me and the balloon envelope. On the next flight he picked up Jan and Aden and more of the equipment, but Chris, Phil and Brian would have to sit it out another night in the mountains. It took three days to air-lift out all the salvageable material. *Zanussi*'s envelope had so many trees sticking up through it, there was no way of saving it, but Chris was anxious to recover as much of the rest of the gear as we could. He was still hoping to make that one last flight we had promised ourselves.

When we were all together once more, I tried to interview Brian to find out more about *Zanussi*'s landing. He was somewhat light-headed now it was all

8 *overleaf:* Drifting silently across the roof of the world in an open wicker basket. In the distance is Makalu (27,825 ft).

over and I had difficulty getting him to be serious for more than a few minutes at a time.

'Why did you have to come down so soon?' I asked him.

'We didn't.'

'What do you mean you didn't? You finished up in the same valley as us.'

'We didn't have to. We had two cylinders left – enough to get us into the next valley, though not much further. The next valley, we could see, was full of active cumulus and this one looked rather more hospitable than it turned out to be. It's sheer chance we landed so close to you; we thought we'd pop down, try and get a lower valley-wind and maybe just manage to make it down to the first village. Ballsed it up, though!'

'What then?' I asked.

'God, it was frightening!' he replied. Jan, it appeared, was the only one able to get out, which she did, fast. Phil had his arms free, but was trapped inside, and poor Brian was upside down on his back, completely stuck with all the baggage on top of him.

'That was when the burner came full on. We'd turned off the pilot lights on landing, of course, but either one just lingered slightly on, or more likely, my head hit the strikers . . . anyway the gas came full on, and burned for about 20 seconds before I could get a hand free to turn it off.'

With two gas cylinders aboard they were lucky not to have gone up like a bomb. Jan began beating out flames with her hands and Phil, half-in, half-out of the basket, tried to get himself out.

'One corner of the basket was badly burned,' Brian continued, 'my rucksack was burned, my duffelbag sort of melted, Jan's jacket was completely melted and her hands were blistered. Quite a blaze! If she hadn't put it out in those first few seconds, the balloon would certainly have caught alight and I would have been incinerated.'

'Didn't you have fire extinguishers?'

'Yes, but nobody could reach them. With the whole bloody basket upside down, there was no way in the world of getting to them. Certainly, I couldn't with my arms pinned to my sides.'

I knew Jan's reputation as an all-round sportswoman. Extremely strong, she skis and climbs with competitive drive, and is not one to accept that men enjoy any physiological advantage over women. The year before our balloon trip she had made an impressive cross-country journey on ski and foot around Everest with fellow-American Ned Gillette. A 'circumperambulation' they called it, but it was by no means as tame as that sounds. They had begun by making the first winter ascent of Pumori, one of Everest's satellite peaks.

Now Jan was making her living as an action-photographer; our ballooning trip was just one of the missions she had been despatched to cover for *National Geographic*, despite having never been up in a balloon before. I had already marked her down as one very determined lady, but had not guessed that her hidden secret lay, as Brian now reliably informed me, in an extraordinarily slow pulse-rate. Jan had told me that Brian experienced trouble with his oxygen apparatus during the flight. I asked him about this.

'Oh darling,' he clowned, 'it was awful! There I was at 21,000 feet gasping for breath, but not being very bright, I never actually thought it was anything to do with the oxygen set. I just kept thinking, Gosh, this air's awfully thick up here and I'm having to breathe an awful lot to get any of it.'

It was Phil who noticed Brian's oxygen tube had fallen out, it was just hanging there, dribbling out the little beads of life-giving air! Phil plugged him in again, and Brian immediately sprang back into normal intelligent life.

'"Jeez, Phil," I said, "you're right! Got any sticky?"'

'Any what?'

'Got any sticky. Sticky tape, you know. Gaffer. We taped it all up, but two minutes later it happened again, and two minutes after that, at which stage we turned over the mask and read Made in Australia. All that messing about cost us about 5,000 feet. Without that, we'd have got higher undoubtedly.'

Ten days later, Chris, Brian and I were ready to have another go. The weather forecast was right, so we booked the helicopter and headed out for Ghandrung, a pretty little village on a steep hillside overlooking Machhapuchhare. This time we planned to fly across the beautiful Annapurna range. Machhapuchhare is a sacred mountain to the Nepalese; its summit must remain untrodden forever in deference to the gods, and no climber these days is even allowed to attempt it. But, as Chris said, there is no ban on flying over it.

We landed beside the village basketball pitch in the late afternoon. There was just enough time to prepare the balloon and basket before turning in for the night in a nearby guesthouse. Three watchmen were hired to guard the equipment, but when we returned at 4.30 the next morning, there was nothing to be heard from them but snoring, and it took a loud shout to bring our sentries back to life! We eventually took off two hours later, just before dawn. I was still fiddling with cameras and only realized we were on our way when I heard Chris shouting goodbye to all the Nepalese children who had

9 *overleaf:* Nothing could escape my remote cameras

left their beds early for the novelty of seeing this strange flying gasbag. As the balloon cut through the still-cold night air, the Annapurnas to our left were painted in that rosy ethereal glow you get half an hour before the sun comes up. There was very little wind. When we came level with the summit of Machhapuchhare, it was obvious we would be going south, away from it, rather than to the east as we had anticipated. Dawn reached us a good 45 minutes before it lit the village we had left behind. The tips of all the major summits in the Annapurna range flushed a warm pink as our balloon continued to climb.

By now we were using oxygen. Chris, as pilot, was on full flow — it was important to keep him alert — but to conserve supplies Brian decided to use only a restricted supply. I remember Chris remarking that the oxygen seemed to be working fine this time, which was odd since we could see that the delivery pipe was dangling uselessly around his knees! Brian quickly plugged him in again, but was himself becoming hypoxic. He could read the compass bearings all right, but was incapable of translating them into any sort of flight plan. I noticed that my feet were growing cold and began stomping around in the bottom of the basket. It was hardly surprising we should be feeling chilly at 25,000 feet, the height of Annapurna itself. At one with the elements, we were seeing the mountains as no man had seen them before. Being in an aeroplane or a helicopter gives nothing like the same sensation as rocking in an open basket at the mercy of the winds. Some of the

10   Our second flight past Machhapuchhare. All Himalayan journeys should be made by balloon.

11 'Which one is Everest?' Chris points out a few famous mountains to Brian as Leo nonchalantly takes a snap.

mountains to the north had plumes of blown snow pouring over the top, and I wondered idly how much curl-over effect would be created some miles downwind of them. We were not in the wind-shadow of any of the big mountains, luckily, but riding in parallel to them, out of reach of such turbulence.

For the first half-hour of the flight, my remote-control camera was pointing the wrong way, with its back to the mountains because of our changed course, and I was helpless to do anything about it. Later, when the balloon began to gyrate, I took advantage of the opportunity and switched on the suspended camera to film the mountains which now looked so close. Meanwhile, I was glad I had connected a battery heater to my hand-held Photosonic for I felt sure that otherwise it would have frozen up. As you would expect, water in the film emulsion freezes when the temperature drops below zero and at around −20°C the emulsion cracks, rendering the film useless. This had happened to me many years ago when I was filming on the North Face of the Matterhorn in winter, but I hoped the effect of the 100-watt heater would be enough to compensate this time.

I leaned out and filmed Dhaulagiri away to the west − and lost the lens hood and filter over the side. 'Damn! Here we go again,' I muttered to myself.

We seemed set on a steady course for Tibet rather than heading back towards Kathmandu and would again have to curtail our flight well before the distance we had planned. After two hours' flying we began the descent just to the south of Lamjung Himal. Then, without warning, that noise began again. Or rather, the lack of it. Once more the burners had blown out, leaving just the feeble hiss of the gas jets. This time it was far more serious. We were over high ground, and only a couple of hundred feet above a steep ridge. Far too low to parachute out. If we came down here, we would surely hit the crest of the ridge and then fall thousands of feet down to the river below.

We escaped by the skin of our teeth. Chris brought the balloon into the sun and the solar effect caused it to rise gently, just long enough for the pilot lights to be relit. Now, if we wanted to land properly, we had to get back into the shade and start going down the valley. Unless we lost more altitude, it would be impossible for our helicopter to come and retrieve us and we would be faced with a long trek out.

I was still filming and saw a lovely composition of our own shadow against the grassy tree-covered slopes, but before I could get a long-enough shot we were back in shadow once more. Chris brought the balloon in to land among the rhododendrons on a 45° slope. There were sharp branches sticking out everywhere and it was difficult to avoid them. The envelope was still upright above us although we were down inside the splintering tree cover. Brian jumped out with the crown line and Chris attempted to ease us out of the trees with a quick burst on the burner. All he succeeded in doing was to set light to the dry wood. History repeated itself. Embers began to rain down into the basket and once more we faced the horror of a fire on landing. Chris immediately switched off the burner and began getting rid of smouldering twigs. Clutching my camera in one hand, I grabbed the fire extinguisher with the other and stood ready to take aim wherever needed. Just then, the balloon performed a surprising lift out of the trees and lurched fifty feet before coming to an abrupt and skewed halt on the awkward slope.

The flight was over. In a few hours, we had the balloon deflated and into its bag, the cylinders derigged and all our bits and pieces packed up before the helicopter located us. It took a couple of trips to get us out, but later that same afternoon we were back in Kathmandu, celebrating our safe return and drinking to the end of the expedition.

2 • HIGH FLYERS

Not long after our Himalayan adventure, I became involved, albeit obliquely, with another major ballooning enterprise. At that time the Atlantic had never been crossed by hot-air balloon – and to be the first to achieve such a feat was the ambition of a number of the world's best hot-air balloonists.

Helium-filled gas balloons had already made long ocean flights (including three across the Atlantic), but these do not pose the same problems as those charged purely with hot air. In good conditions, a gas balloon can remain aloft almost indefinitely (or until a critical percentage of the gas has seeped through the near-impermeable fabric); a hot-air balloon on the other hand relies for its lift on the air inside the envelope being permanently warmer than that outside. Hence the burners. If they blow out, then the balloon descends very quickly (as ours did in Nepal), yet keeping them alight on a long or turbulent journey is not easy. Also, the longer the distance to be travelled, the more fuel is needed; and the more fuel you decide to take, the bigger your balloon has to be to carry it. It is easy to see why 3,000 miles of ocean present such a formidable challenge to hot-air balloons.

Per Lindstrand, a Swedish-born balloonist from Oswestry, was one whose sights were set on a transatlantic crossing. A few years earlier he had made an abortive bid for the world hot-air altitude record: before assembled newsmen, his balloon had billowed and burst without even leaving the ground. Lindstrand himself was hoisted ignobly into the air and, tumbling back down, had broken a wrist. The Sunday papers were unkind: 'One giant let-down for mankind', they blazoned.

Finding sponsorship for a large-scale project is always difficult, especially if you are obliged to acknowledge earlier failures. A number of gas balloons in the early transatlantic attempts had ditched in the ocean, with several of the balloonists being killed. A hot-air crossing was no less likely to founder, and what sponsor wants to be associated with disaster? Per Lindstrand's stroke of fortune was to meet up with the young and energetic tycoon

12 In the company of Nick Harrison, Richard Branson and Sharkey Sheridan

Richard Branson, for whom the Atlantic already exercised a powerful attraction. The success of Branson's Virgin-Atlantic airline had brought him fame and prosperity; his speedy powerboat crossing in quest of the Blue Riband had stimulated a latent urge for adventure. Provided he could fly with Lindstrand, Branson was prepared, indeed enthusiastic, to back an attempt to make the first transatlantic hot-air balloon flight.

Richard Branson had never previously flown in a balloon, and quickly had to acquire sufficient experience not to be a liability on the trip. The pair were to travel in a pressurized capsule loaded with all the latest electronic safety equipment but, as a further precaution, had been advised to take parachutes. Skydiving was something else Branson had not attempted before; he asked me to arrange a course of training for him.

The old idea of beginners first making static-line jumps is fast disappearing. These days, they can be given an immediate idea of what the sport is all about by the revolutionary learning technique called Accelerated Freefall. It was invented in Florida in the early 1980s: a student jumps with two very experienced jumpers, who hold on to him for 50 long seconds until his parachute is safely open. It's hard to imagine but they fall for almost two miles. I arranged for my friends Sharky Sheridan and Nick Harrison to be Branson's instructors.

On the ground, he was a model student, light on his feet and seemingly quick to absorb theory. Our problems started when we got him into the air. At 13,000 feet I reached out of the door and hung on to the side of the aircraft, waiting for the other three. I would jump with them and capture on film Richard's first exciting seconds of freefall. In the plane he had appeared very relaxed and keen to make the jump, but there was a long delay in the doorway while he got Sharky to run through procedures one last time. Eventually they made a perfect launch.

Ten seconds later, Richard curled himself into a tight ball and tumbled over and over and over. They were anxious moments for the instructors who were trying to control him, but then, as he had been taught, he pulled the ripcord to open his canopy and floated down safely. It was the only time he managed to do so. On three subsequent jumps he failed to find the handle, and on each occasion Sharky had to pull it for him. This is one of the safety nets of accelerated freefall, though one's in-built survival instincts mean it is rarely used. Richard seemed to be placing too much trust in his instructors.

On his fifth jump, anxious to please, he did grab and pull a handle – but

13   *below left:* With his right hand firmly on the red pad, novice Branson practised 'cutting away' his main parachute. Sharkey watches with disbelief.
14   *right:* Richard, still grasping the cutaway pad, starts to roll over as his parachute deploys

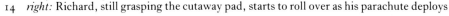

it was the wrong one. Instead of opening his main canopy, Richard cut it away! His parachute was left way behind as he dropped inexorably earthwards.

Luckily, this accelerated learning system is so safe, it is near impossible to die when using it. If neither the student nor the instructor has successfully opened the main chute by the time they are 1,500 feet from the ground, it deploys automatically.

Richard Branson's reserve canopy opened perfectly and he landed with his usual broad grin. I had thought my film dramatic enough, but the papers still overdid it:

Sunday Mail 31 May 1987: TV Review
For those of us sick of wading through jettisoned hamburgers and plucking beer cans from our window boxes, Tuesday brought the week's worst moment. The radiant young minister for litter, upon whom all our environmental hopes rest, leapt from an aeroplane at umpteen thousand feet, and faced with two dangling cords, tugged the wrong one. His parachute fell off. For several plummeting seconds Richard Branson seemed doomed to end up as just one more unsavoury thing for his ministry to shovel off the road. But help, thank God, was at hand. Two madmen dived on him and saved him for the nation.

When their story broke, Virgin's shares fell further than he did, losing £15 million on the stock market!

Per Lindstrand and Richard Branson ultimately crossed the Atlantic, west to east, in their balloon *Virgin Atlantic Flyer*. The flight, however, nearly ended in disaster. Touching down in Northern Ireland, the two men found it impossible to arrest the giant balloon, which merely scraped the ground before rising into the air again and whisking them off over the Irish Sea. Taking their chances, Per and Richard leapt (separately) into the water, from where Naval helicopters fortunately were able to rescue them both.

Neither man used his parachute.

Nobody knows who first came up with the idea for a parachute. More than likely it was the ancient Chinese. There are stories that they used to force prisoners to leap from battlements harnessed to bamboo mats, or with nothing but a parasol to support them, granting freedom to those who survived, but I suspect there were few who did.

Certainly, that great visionary Leonardo da Vinci doodled a primitive parachute in one of his sketchbooks in 1495. It had a pyramidal canopy,

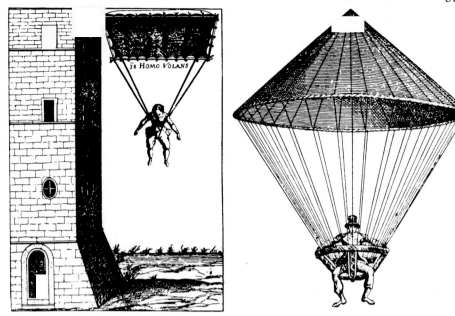

38 HOMO VOLANS

15 *above left:* Fauste Veranzio – the 'Flying Man'
16 *above right:* In 1783 Sebastian Lenormand developed a larger and lighter parachute.
The bent-knee position is still adopted for landing.

beneath which dangled a man supported by lines from each of the four corners. History does not record that Leonardo found a guinea-pig willing to try out the device, but a few years ago NASA put a number of his inventions to the test and proved them practicable, the parachute among them. Scale models made from his drawings can be seen at the house in Amboise in France where he passed the last years of his life, and which is now a museum dedicated to his fabulous machines.

Leonardo had been dead for almost a hundred years before matters progressed any further. In 1617, a Venetian eccentric by the name of Fauste Veranzio fashioned a square-framed parachute from wood and canvas, and with it leapt boldly from a belfry near his home. He landed with a thud, but in one piece, and *Homo volans* (Flying Man), as he chose to call himself, was born. More time had to pass, however, before others were tempted to follow his example.

It was the advent of ballooning that led to the first serious interest in parachuting during the second half of the eighteenth century. Early balloons were made of paper or fabric, and to keep their shape they were supported upon a framework of rigid spars. Sometimes, when a balloon failed (and this was not uncommon), part of the fabric would catch around the spars and create a kind of involuntary parachute, slowing down its rate of fall. It was enough to inspire inventors to develop the idea; an alternative means of descent if anything happened to the balloon was clearly desirable. One French balloonist, Jean-Pierre Blanchard, who was something of a showman, travelled Europe dropping dogs and other animals attached to small parachutes in order to demonstrate the effectiveness of the parachuting principle. Although he baulked at trying it himself, he did take the precaution of fitting a parachute canopy, rather like an umbrella, between his balloon envelope and the basket in which he travelled, just in case of emergency.

The day inevitably came when he was called upon to put his precautionary device to the test. In November 1785 at 1,500 feet the pressure in his balloon suddenly rose so alarmingly that it threatened to explode. It would be too late then for his umbrella to save him – everything, Blanchard included, – would be blown to pieces. Something had to be done! Seizing his flagstaff, Blanchard punctured the balloon. Watchers on the ground saw it deflate and begin plunging downwards. Frantically, Blanchard cut away at the ropes securing the useless balloon to the basket. Once free of its encumbrance, his patent parachute was able to arrest his fall and bring him safely back to earth without a scratch.

Within a few years another Frenchman, André Jacques Garnerin, had produced an improved model with which he intended to jump from even

17 André Jacques Garnerin bails out over the Parc Monceau in Paris. Modern display teams still wave flags.

greater heights. It had no supporting framework and he proposed trailing it, uninflated, beneath his balloon. Late in the afternoon of 22 October 1797, he rose bravely into the air above the Parc Monceau in Paris, watched by an eager crowd of spectators. Above the city, Garnerin attained a height of 2,300 feet before calmly cutting the lines that held basket and parachute to the balloon.

For a long, heart-stopping moment, Garnerin plummeted earthwards, just as Blanchard had done, with his parachute streaming in a useless bundle behind him. Then, miraculously, the fabric billowed and filled with air. Though his fall was checked, Garnerin swung violently beneath the canopy like a crazy pendulum. What he had not appreciated when designing his masterpiece was that he needed to build into it some method, some chimney, by which the air collected in descent could be spilled out safely. The further he fell, the wilder became the oscillations, so that by the time he landed he was feeling extremely sick. But nothing could spoil his triumph. The admiring crowd hoisted him shoulder-high and paraded him jubilantly around the capital. Today, if you go to the Allée Garnerin in Paris, named in his honour, you should still be able to find the commemorative plaque placed there to mark the historic landing.

Garnerin had a young niece, Elisa, who shared his daredevil streak. Once he had modified his design to provide a smoother ride, the 'Beautiful Elisa' made more than forty exhibition jumps before delighted crowds. Others, too, were quick to take up the sensational new activity, and ever more spectacular stunts were performed in the air. Throughout Europe, no fair or festival was complete without its parachute jumpers.

Parachuting was regarded merely as a form of entertainment, and continued so throughout the nineteenth century. Attempts were made to improve design, not all of them successful, and there were several fatalities. One particularly bull-headed Englishman, a man called Cocking, took himself into an evolutionary dead-end when he conceived the inverted canopy. It resembled nothing more than a brolly that had blown inside-out, but he convinced himself it was about to revolutionize parachuting. Nothing anybody said could persuade him otherwise. One day in July 1837, his invention proudly strapped to his shoulders, he stepped from a balloon more than 6,000 feet in the air and fell, of course, to his death.

Modifications of a more practical nature were made in the years that followed. The practice of packing a parachute to minimize entangling was adopted; this enabled a reserve chute to be carried as well, and prepared the jumper for cutting away the main canopy in the event of malfunction. By the First World War, a few jumps had been made from aeroplanes rather than balloons, though it was not until the German engineer Heinecke invented a static line that this could be done with any degree of safety. The line, attached to the plane, granted the jumper precious moments to clear its bodywork before automatically opening the canopy. In 1914 a young American parachutist, Georgina 'Tiny' Broadwick, jumped holding her own static line, to pull when she felt the moment was ripe. Freefall parachuting was born.

With the advent of aerial warfare, there was interest in designing parachutes strong enough to save precious aircraft when they were shot down. Not surprisingly, this proved futile, and it was only then that attention shifted to their usefulness in saving pilots. The Germans were the first to issue their airmen with parachutes; the Royal Flying Corps dragged its heels until the very end of the war. Parachutes were considered by them to be rather ungentlemanly, not quite cricket, and in consequence some 6,000 British pilots lost their lives during the First World War. The enemy did not sustain anything like such heavy losses.

In 1919 in McCook's Field, Ohio, there was widespread publicity for a freefall jump made by one Leslie L. Irvin employing a delayed-opening device. Its success was instrumental in having the parachute universally accepted as a life-saving apparatus. One to benefit from the development was American aviator Charles Lindbergh; he employed parachutes to save his life no less than four times. Without them he would never have survived long enough to make his celebrated solo crossing of the Atlantic!

At the start of the Second World War the Russians were capable of dropping a division of men by parachute, although the first practical use of airborne invasion was by the Germans in their Blitzkrieg on Holland and Belgium in 1940; this they followed with the invasion of Crete the following year. The idea of dropping airborne troops behind enemy lines had first been mooted by an American soldier at the end of the First World War – yet the British were surprisingly slow to appreciate the usefulness of a specialized parachute force. It took the German successes to convince them. In 1941 the Central Landing School was established at Ringway Airport in Manchester for the training of British airborne troops. The first jumps were made from the back of Whitley bombers using a 'pull-off' technique. This involved standing at an open hatchway, deploying the parachute, and waiting for it to inflate. The shock of opening was sufficient to yank the soldier into the air. Not long afterwards, the Special Air Service was formed

18   *above:* Two abreast!
19   *below:* Blowing in the wind. Wally Gubbins and Ian Head skyjiving over the Mediterranean.

and in 1942 began dropping sabotage teams into North Africa, by now using static-line rigs.

By D-Day, parachuting had become firmly established as a strategic means of delivering troops and equipment to the battle zone. For the attack on Arnhem and the other Rhine bridges later in 1944, more than thirty thousand men were dropped by parachute or glider into German-occupied territory, and although losses were heavy and the bridgehead at Arnhem was not secured, this will be remembered as one of the greatest airborne assaults of all time.

After the war, a vast surplus of parachute equipment found its way on to the open market, and of the several thousand people trained to make jumps, there were many who wished to continue parachuting in a civilian capacity. This provided the impetus for sport parachuting. No longer was jumping merely the means of getting people quickly to the ground, it could be enjoyed and perfected for its own sake. There evolved a greater understanding of the dynamics of freefall. An Italian diver, Salvator Canarrozzo, discovered how to cleave the air in a head-down position that gave great stability, if little comfort. Sad to relate, Canarrozzo, like so many of the sport's pioneers, was killed when his parachute failed to open one day.

Next came Leo Valentin, a champion jumper of the French Air Force, who, from observing how different objects sank in water, devised the arched body position that is still adopted in freefall today. Its chief advantages are stability and manoeuvrability; at the same time it opened the way to formation-building and relative work. Flying in freefall, unfortunately, was not enough for Valentin. His heart's desire was to glide like a bird. To this end, he experimented first with webbed canvas wings, and then rigid wooden ones, attached to his chest and arms. In one test over France in May 1954 he succeeded in 'flying' for more than three miles, but not long afterwards, he crashed to his death in Liverpool before a crowd of almost 100,000 who had come to watch the world-famous Bird Man in action.

With official recognition of parachuting as a sport in 1954, competitions were instigated to test accuracy and style, and later, relative work. Relative work is the linking up of bodies in freefall. At first this meant holding hands in round formations, but nowadays any number of patterns can be 'built', and it is best, I think, to consider the activity a form of sky dancing.

Inevitably, as the sport progressed, people began to play the numbers

20 *opposite:* The opening cord
21 *overleaf:* A new world record in the making

game, to see just how many people could be linked together in the sky at any one time. A NASA scientist put forward the theory that if 180 people ever linked together in freefall, such would be the drag they would create, they could land without any need of opening their parachutes! Well, we're still a way from knowing if that is true or not, and I don't suppose we will ever find anyone to put it to the test! Rarely do large formations hold together for more than a few seconds.

When I started jumping seriously ten years ago, the largest formations being built were of about sixty people, but with the sport increasing in popularity all the time, this was quickly improved upon; by the mid eighties people were already talking of the Magic Hundred. A major handicap to large numbers jumping together has always been finding the means of delivering them into position. Few planes can launch more than forty divers, and even then, tumbling in close succession out of the door, the last diver will be leaving the plane a good while after the first, and in a different part of the sky. For them to come together in the air requires a lot of holding back on the part of the first divers, and a lot of hasty swooping by the last. In theory it hardly seems to work at all, not when you consider falling speeds: the first jumpers could well be over a thousand feet below the aeroplane and falling at over 100 mph while others are still waiting to leave, but certain ploys are exercised to minimize the effects of this.

It takes about ten seconds in freefall to reach 'terminal velocity' of 120

22   At break-off time I flew beneath the group to watch them separate

23   *above:* Looking down a big stack of Royal Marines. Greg Andrew seems to be
     enjoying it.
24   *overleaf:* The last jump of the day and a new world record of 23 parachutes all stacked
     together. Eventually they got 24.

mph. Divers can only go faster by altering their wind resistance in some way.
By 'standing' on their heads, and diving for instance, and thus reducing the
slipstream to a minimum, speeds of up to 200 mph can be reached. In this
way, later divers can streak like comets to catch comrades who left the plane
earlier. It is important, of course, for them to slow down again in good time
(by 'flaring out' into a spreadeagled position), otherwise they could go
screaming past. With a difference in speed of anything up to 80 mph, it is
easy to see how serious a collision could be. People have been killed in
mid-air direct hits. The mechanics of any formation dive have to be
meticulously planned, and the whole thing practised to perfection by
repetitive 'dirt dives' on the ground first.

One way of telescoping exit time is for half a dozen 'floaters' to clamber
onto the outside of the aeroplane and cling to handles on the fuselage, so that
eventually they can let go and fall together.

The base of a formation is built by the first divers out whose job it is to
hold steady and maintain a good 'ground heading'. They must stay facing in
one direction and not allow themselves to drift around. Each diver has an
allotted position that he must fly straight into; he cannot just 'dock'
anywhere, and the ground heading saves confusion.

On one jump I filmed in the centre of a record-attempt of over 100 people. With three cameras and a bulky flying-suit, I could not hope to match their speed. My aim was to 'park' on one of the skydivers until the formation had slowed sufficiently for me to stay with it, leaving me free to spin around within the central circle. No one had ever tried this before and it involved a certain amount of trust from my fellow skydivers.

Inside this sea of human motion, the impressions are kaleidoscopic. Some people are concentrating intently, others smiling contentedly. It is all like a gigantic hologram, a phantom. The formation is there, suspended in space, for fleeting moments only; then it is gone. Looking around at everyone for those split seconds when the earth is rushing towards you at 120 mph, you know you are all really dead. You cannot just linger in space. Provided you pull out your parachutes, you live again. It is that simple. Perhaps this is the attraction of freefall: you can build imagery that is at the same time real and unreal, truth yet fiction, an abstract, living dream.

Traditionally, all record attempts at large formations have taken place in North America where there are plenty of privately-owned DC-3s capable of carrying enough people. When going for a hundred, you need three of these capacious old warhorses to spill everyone into the sky together. As the years pass, however, they have become increasingly whimsical, with a provoking habit of breaking down just as everybody is keyed up for the final 'jump run'. These days, it is more usual for a combination of old and newer, turbine aircraft to be used. In the spring of 1986 in Vancouver, two DC-3s and one Twin Otter put a hundred skydivers in the air, as well as the usual complement of aerial cameramen (including myself) to record the event.

We had wanted to jump out at 15,000 feet, which would have given us ample time to scuttle into position, but Canadian Air Traffic Control limited us to 12,000 feet only. (They needed the extra airspace for jets approaching Vancouver International Airport.) Consequently, as we came in for our first jump run, there was a general air of frustration and nobody felt our 100-way attempt stood the remotest chance of success. Tom Piras, the organizer, had decreed that 5,000 feet was the altitude at which the attempt was to be broken off. People would then track away to find an empty bit of sky in which to open their chutes safely. As a cameraman, my position was to be just above all the activity, giving me a good overall view of the formation as it built. When my altimeter was reading 5,500 feet, I was surprised to see the hundredth skydiver come in to join the others. Once back on the ground, we all rushed to see the videos to discover whether the formation had held for

25   A giant caterpillar flies through the skies

the qualifying three seconds. Alas, it was plain from our pictures that as the last diver docked others on the opposite side were already beginning to leave. If only we had gone down to 4,500 feet, the record would have been ours at our very first attempt! Though we tried several more times during the week, we never managed to link more than 98 or 99 people.

Perhaps the Magic Hundred, which I had been so eager to film, was impossible after all. By now, there had been several all-out attempts, but that first three-digit jump was steadfastly elusive. The problems, however, were becoming clearer. Wind resistance seemed to be the key. Later divers can be given larger jump suits with winged sleeves to create more drag, while those at the base of the formation wear skinny suits to reduce theirs, but it is hardly an exact science. And with so many people in the air, there are more opportunities for human error.

On one attempt in Illinois, there was a serious mid-air collision between two divers who had come out of the same plane. One was knocked unconscious and fell limply on to his back. Three others immediately gave chase, hoping to be able to pull his ripcord for him, but it was a forlorn hope. The manoeuvre has only been done once or twice successfully. Luckily, the plummeting man regained consciousness in time to turn over and deploy his own parachute, but it was a very close call.

A couple of weeks after I returned from Vancouver, the American National Championships were held, at which Tom Piras and Guy Manos organized yet another attempt at the record. This time they were successful. Not only did 100 people link together, but they held the formation for a good six seconds, three longer than was necessary for an official record. I was sorry to have missed it, and felt sure that, with the effort and finance involved, it would mark the end of the major record-breaking bids. Boogies would go back to being lighthearted events for sheer fun, not given over to such intense competition. After all, we would never see a 200-way. Would we?

I was writing it all off too soon. Roger Nelson at his Freakbrother Convention of 1986 changed all the ground rules. He was bidding for the 120, and to make sure of it he had brought in a C-130 Hercules from South Africa, capable of lifting 140 skydivers at one time! The day of the DC-3 with its awkward side-door was definitely over. Skydivers could leave a Hercules eight-abreast; 120 could be pitched outside within 8 seconds and, provided oxygen was used, jumps could be made from 20,000 feet. With much longer dives to look forward to, skydivers were ecstatic.

26 A Biplane Diamond conveniently suspended from a chopper

27   The Olympic Ring skydive in Spain

Breaking the record became almost a formality. Perhaps this, then, was where it would stick – 120 – or was the sky truly the limit?

Two Belgian parachutists, Didier Lagasse and Etienne Hérin, had been secretly working on a Belgium Air Show to take place in the summer of 1987. With inspired optimism they approached the Belgian Air Force for not one, but two, C-130 aircraft. The fact that the Belgian Air Force seemed to possess only two C-130s made it all the more remarkable that they succeeded in getting them!

The next problem was to find enough good skydivers who would dedicate time to a record attempt organized by people of whom they had never heard. Didier and Etienne had decided this was to be a truly European attempt and invitations were sent out to qualifying jumpers. Mandy, my wife, was asked to take part and I to be in charge of the aerial filming. The goal was 126.

Our first attempt built to 99, which was tremendous for morale. Few of the people had jumped together before, or indeed been in any really large formations. Over the week we improved this to 110, 112, 119 – all new figures for the European scene. Our optimism soared.

Then late one evening, with a red sun shimmering over the water of the English Channel, it almost happened. From my vantage point above the building star, I found myself holding my breath as this large, flat, flying object steadily grew before my eyes, with scarcely a ripple to destroy its symmetry. Mandy flew in front of me, hugging the camera limelight for a glimpse in time, as she made her way to her designated position. 124 jumpers, from all over Europe and the USA, linked together in one gigantic 'megablob'. It held for an extraordinary 14 seconds, during which time it fell over half a mile. Two did not make their slots, but it hardly seemed to matter. That night everyone was elated at this new 'unofficial' record, but next morning would be our last chance to get it absolutely right. Perhaps because everyone was more relaxed, it went like clockwork. We jumped at 20,000 feet, dived down a couple of miles and watched. This time the last few divers all flew in safely and, suddenly, we had 126 people clasped together in one intricate, beautiful skimming snowflake. The world record was ours! It was the first time it had ever left the United States.

There were some frantic transatlantic telephone calls over the next few days, seeking verification for an outrageous claim that was coming out of Belgium. People simply did not believe it. Where could 126 skydivers have come from? Someone suggested ringing up the White House and asking to borrow three Hercules aircraft to restore American pride.

Clearly, the Americans will get their record back, not least because they have the largest reserve of experienced skydivers and they almost all speak the same language, but also because they are so much better at winning than losing.

Where will it all end? I am sure that shortly we shall see 150 people in the sky. We will pass the NASA-man's symbolic 180 – although I guess we'll still be using our parachutes – and perhaps within a year or two, we will even reach 200. From there on, it's fantasy, but I know where there is a large balloon gathering dust on a factory shelf. It is the one Don Cameron designed to take four of us around the world, but which for one reason or another, never took to the skies. I think to myself sometimes, supposing it were allowed to fly, supposing we filled it with 300 skydivers and took them up to 15,000 feet. And then, just supposing, they were all to jump out simultaneously! Could the balloon, the earliest flying machine of all, the inspiration of the first parachutes, be the means of giving us a world record that could never be broken?

3 • HARLIN'S EIGER FALL

'The only way to stage a long fall on screen, and have it look at all realistic', I said, 'is to use a *real* body falling!'

I was giving Fred Zinnemann the benefit of my advice, but he didn't seem to be rising to my enthusiasm. We were on location in the Swiss Alps for the shooting of the famous director's last film, *Five Days One Summer*. The plot called for Sean Connery, the hero, and Lambert Wilson, the mountain guide who in the film is his rival in love, to be caught in a rockfall while out climbing together. On impact, one of them – and the audience is not immediately allowed to know which – falls to his death a couple of thousand feet down the mountainside. Zinnemann proposed to use a dummy for the fall, and, to be on the safe side, had two made in case he did not get what he wanted first time. They were dressed identically to the victim – who is later revealed to be the young guide, not Connery – and were so realistic that a couple of times when I saw one lying out on the glacier, I thought I had surprised Lambert snatching a quick snooze on set. Even so, I knew they would never fool anybody when 'performing' the actual scene. I persisted.

'No, I mean it! No matter how lifelike you make the dummy, once you drop it off a cliff, it's going to look like a rag doll.'

'So, what are you saying? No stunt man will buy a fall of several hundred feet. Are you crazy?'

'No, no, you don't understand. What you need is a parachutist! You could have him freefall down in front of the mountain.'

I could see it clearly. We would need a skydiver with sufficient experience to fly upside down to give the impression of falling, and the parachute pack on his back would need to be disguised as a rucksack. Strangely, Zinnemann (Mr Zee as everyone called him) remained unconvinced. His shots were already planned and, so far as he could see, my idea could well prove no more than an expensive diversion that failed to produce what was wanted.

In any case, it sounded highly dangerous, and he already had enough to worry about on that score with the climbing. Some of Britain's best climbers had been hired to act as safety officers, and if he were to stage the fall my way, there would have to be a similar crew of top skydivers. So, he stuck to his dummies. They were eventually tossed out of a helicopter against different mountain backdrops until there was enough material to build up the required accident sequence. I was left with a feeling of wasted opportunity.

If I had been unsuccessful in persuading Mr Zee even to give my idea a try, I had done a pretty good job of convincing myself! So sure was I that it would work, I determined to put it to the test myself, and soon. Already I could see a chance to use it.

The film I had shot the year before of Eric Jones's solo ascent of the Eiger had still not been put together. I was anxious to get it just right and had not rushed into editing because there were still a few things that worried me. Heart-stopping as I had found it to watch Eric inching his way up the mountain without ropes, I knew that viewed in the comfort of a stranger's living room, without all those atmospheric rustles and rumbles, without the wind and cold or the mountain's damp smell, and more especially without the uncertainty of the outcome and the fear that any slip could be his last, Eric's climb would inevitably lose impact. I doubted if a lone figure making his introspective way upwards could sustain an hour's programme. It could, of course, be trimmed down to half that, but at what cost! It would diminish Eric's achievement and emasculate the mountain. No, I needed to find some way of conveying the Eiger's vastness, its allure and its grim history, a way of putting Eric and his climb into sharp perspective.

On one level you could say that the Eiger, like any other mountain, is no more than a variable compound of geology and weather. Yet, true as that is, combined in the hollow scoop of its North Face these ingredients frequently produce so explosive a reaction that it seems a malignant force must be at work, some fearful power which lies in wait to lash out at anyone who dares draw near. And because this North Face, the *Eigerwand*, hangs like a gigantic movie-screen above the tourist villages of the Grindelwald valley, no climb upon its slopes can ever be a private affair. Enterprising hotel owners long ago realized there was money to be earned from telescopes trained on its icy precipices. Eiger-climbing has been likened to gladiatorial combat, and not without cause. From the mid-thirties, the world has been

29   Ron Fawcett reconstructing the Eiger Direct climb

watching. When the first two, then the next four climbers all died — either with abrupt violence or in protracted agony — press cameras clicked, pundits pronounced, and the ghouls devoured the pieces! A monster was created. A myth. Eiger fever was born.

Unfortunately the tragedies did not stop even after the *Eigerwand* was at last successfully climbed in 1938 by Anderl Heckmair, Wiggerl Vörg, Heinrich Harrer and Fritz Kasparek. The mountain acquired a notoriety that it shares with no other, so that now there is no way of separating myth from reality, certainly no way of severing the mountain from its macabre history. Anyone who climbs the Eiger cannot but be aware of it. To go up there, you have to trample over its legends and consort with its ghosts.

It was something of this mythic aura that I wanted to get into my film. I wanted the audience to know just what Eric was up against, and to have some idea of the attempts that had preceded his. I wanted them to appreciate how — even when you know that so much written about the Eiger is over-sensationalized — it is still impossible to set off up its North Wall without a presentiment of foreboding.

Where vintage film and photographs exist, they can be used to conjure up the essence of history; but where they do not, the film-maker is left with few options but to stage a reconstruction of events — a technique I've always liked. Some years ago we had great fun doing it for my Matterhorn film to show Whymper's first ascent in 1865 and the terrible disaster that befell his party on the way down. Not only does it prove effective, but there is an unexpected by-product: re-enacting past events often throws up inconsistencies. As with a police reconstruction, new clues can emerge: at the very least, you are helped towards a better appreciation of events and the factors leading up to them.

Reconstructions were going to be the most appropriate way of handling at least some of my Eiger history since the photographic record is decidedly sketchy. The only climbing film I knew to exist (besides my own of 1970) was one shot by Toni Hiebeler on 8mm during the first winter ascent of the early sixties. I was amused to discover that Chris Brasher must have been similarly frustrated by the lack of authentic archive material when he was making a BBC film about the Eiger some years ago, for he used helicopter shots of four men reaching the summit taken from Hiebeler's 1961 winter climb in conjunction with a commentary describing the first ascent in the summer of 1938! Viewers were certainly given the impression that it was Heckmair and his party they were seeing. Perhaps it was acceptable film-maker's licence, but it was not how I wanted to do it.

However best illustrated — whether by using old photographs, or interviewing survivors, by reconstruction, or, indeed, by any combination of these — I had to select those historical incidents which were essential to the Eiger myth. Two men from the first ascent were, I knew, still alive — Anderl Heckmair and Heinrich Harrer — I would need to interview them. At the same time, there was no doubt in my mind that an episode crying out to be included was John Harlin's bold but disastrous attempt at a direct assault up the middle of the North Face.

People often say they can remember exactly what they were doing when they heard the news that President Kennedy had been assassinated. For mountaineers, it was a bit like that when John Harlin fell down the Eiger. The year was 1966 and I was an engineering student in Preston. We were listening to the lecturer's transistor radio in the college workshop when programmes were interrupted by a news flash about Harlin's death. I still remember the shock of that announcement as if it happened yesterday.

Few climbs have attracted as much attention as the 'race' that took place for the route known as Eiger Direct. This almost straight line from the foot of the North Face to the Eiger summit had fixed itself in John Harlin's mind as the most aesthetically perfect route on the mountain, and he made no secret about his wish to be the first to climb it; he had already climbed the beautiful, but meandering classic line put up by Heckmair's party in 1938.

Harlin surveyed 'his' *direttissima* from a helicopter and made three reconnaissance climbs before he felt ready for a full-scale assault. In the middle of February 1966, with his chosen companions, fellow-American Layton Kor and Scots climber Dougal Haston, Harlin was poised at Kleine Scheidegg at the foot of the North Face, ready to go as soon as conditions allowed. Suddenly, unannounced, a strong eight-man German party entered the arena. The duel was on. Throughout the rest of that month and most of the next, the two teams pushed up, retreated, and pushed up again, first one holding the advantage, then the other — and all the while newsmen gathered in ever greater numbers to follow their progress.

Covering the story for the *Daily Telegraph* was a young British journalist, Peter Gillman, who maintained regular radio contact with Harlin throughout the climb and kept tape-recordings of all the conversations he had with him and the other participants. Later he was to draw upon these tapes for the book *Eiger Direct*, which he wrote in collaboration with Dougal Haston, one of the five men who made it to the top after Harlin's death.

Having decided to reconstruct Harlin's climb for my Eiger film, I got in touch with Peter and explained my plans. We were old friends (he had

30   John Harlin and his mountain of destiny

written up my first Patagonian trip for the *Sunday Times*) and he offered to lend me the tapes. In due course, a fat package arrived and I began the task of sorting the material into chronological order from Peter's diary and notes. It was an odd experience, eavesdropping on those conversations of almost 17 years ago. I lost all sense of the present and for days was right back in 1966, except that I retained the knowledge of the way things turned out. How many remarks, regarded with that dimension of hindsight, now seemed poignantly prophetic. Harlin had often been likened to a Greek god on account of his tall, blond good looks and the analogy was perhaps more apt than people knew, for there appears a dramatic inevitability to his life which is worthy of Greek tragedy.

The American invasion of the Alps had started in 1963 when a group of very tough climbers, trained on the granite pillars of Yosemite Valley, were taking Europe by storm, converting their big-wall experience into a swagbag of new, hard routes, which included the Hidden Pillar of Frêney and the Aiguille du Fou. Among them were Royal Robbins, Tom Frost, Gary Hemming and an ex-fighter pilot of striking appearance, John Harlin. Chris Bonington, who met Harlin in France that summer, brought back slides of this well-proportioned hunk muscling his way up Chamonix boulder problems. In 1964 he climbed the West Face of the Blaitière with the French politician Pierre Mazeaud, and the following year he and Royal Robbins made a new direct route on the North Face of the Dru. By this time Harlin had established the International School of Mountaineering at Leysin in Switzerland, and the list of climbers he was able to attract there as lecturers and instructors reads like a roll-call of the internationally famous: Joe Brown, Yves Chouinard, Bev Clarke, André Contamine, René Desmaison, Dougal Haston, Toni Hiebeler, Gaston Rébuffat . . .

Whatever he did, Harlin made news, and as his reputation grew, so too did the aura that surrounded him. Tales of hard-fighting, hard-drinking and womanizing proliferated and, true or not, he did little to discourage them, seeming to revel in the notoriety. He certainly enjoyed the acclaim that came with new hard climbs. 'We don't court publicity,' he used to say, 'but we sure as hell know how to use it.'

By the time of the Eiger Direct climb, he had it down to a fine art. If he were to raise enough money for a sustained attack, he needed to sell his story to the highest bidder and he succeeded in persuading the *Daily Telegraph* to back the whole venture. However, even Harlin could not have foreseen the added interest the German competition would provide. People love a contest. The siege-style tactics both teams were forced to adopt only served to heighten the drama.

Harlin held regular press briefings by radio from a snowhole halfway up the face, and what those daily bulletins were saying, in effect, to anyone that cared to listen, was: 'Come and watch me climb!' Maybe he was dangerously tempting fate, but the possibility of failure never entered Harlin's equations. In all he did, he was used to success. Yet the tensions created after a month of living such an exposed existence, at a constant pitch of nervous energy, practically dictated disaster in the end. In terms of Greek tragedy, it is easy to imagine that the Eiger needed a sacrifice, and that symbolically the sacrifice had to be Harlin, the figure in red, centre-stage, the one who above all others had shouted bold defiance at the gods. It is little wonder that the world's press, having been invited to come and watch, made such a meal of the story when Harlin fell.

Only one person saw John Harlin fall. Peter Gillman happened to be looking through the telescope, panning up the line of fixed ropes to check progress, when a red bundle fell through his field of vision and continued down to the foot of the mountain. He had the vivid sense of arms and legs outstretched as the figure tumbled through the air, and with a sick feeling of certainty, knew it could not have been just a falling rucksack. He trained the telescope along the foot of the face and eventually saw something red in the snow.

Gillman, through his regular radio link-ups, had become very involved in this climb, and very close to Harlin's family and friends during their long vigil at the foot of the mountain. He was clearly shaken when he rushed to tell the news to Bonington and Don Whillans who were staying in the same hotel. People have an in-built safety valve that makes them reluctant to embrace hard truth. Despite Gillman's conviction that some*one* had fallen, Bonington clung to the hope that there might be some less terrible explanation. Nevertheless, after skiing round to the spot, there was the body of Harlin crumpled in the snow. He had fallen four and a half thousand feet after the fixed rope he was climbing broke, just below the White Spider.

It was for this fall, in my reconstruction of Harlin's climb, that I intended to put my parachuting idea into practice. I set about working out what it would entail. The part of the victim would need to be taken by several 'players'. There would have to be a climber climbing prior to the fall; then a skydiver to make the actual fall. If we were to show the body hitting the ground, we would need, as Zinnemann had, some sort of dummy; and finally, there would have to be a close-up of someone lying in the snow.

Steep as it is, the *Eigerwand* is nowhere near vertical, and a falling climber would undoubtedly bounce many times before striking the bottom, but I felt sure that if someone fell down past the mountain, even if in reality they were a couple of hundred feet out from the face, it would give the impression of a real fall. The biggest problem would be persuading a skydiver to freefall on his back; for stability and control, a spread-eagled face-down position is usually adopted. I needed to conduct some experiments, and the only place for these was in Florida, with its guaranteed good weather and unrestricted jumping facilities. I enlisted the help of 'Apples' (Paul Applegate), a skydiving friend, and together we began working out what equipment we would need.

We first had to disguise a parachute as a climbing rucksack. I got hold of two identical rucksacks, one for the climbing-climber and the other to be cut into pieces and remade around a red parachute harness, then discussed the problem with Jim Walmsley, Chief Rigger at Netheravon Parachute Centre, who agreed to do the conversion for me.

'It's different. Quite looking forward to it!' he said.

With ingenuity and a great deal of polystyrene foam, Jim managed to rearrange the parachute and reserve into the dismembered rucksack and make it look pretty convincing; he thoughtfully also included an automatic

31   The White Spider just emerging through the mists at the top centre, with the Third Icefield like a giant movie screen below

opening device in case, as he put it, anything went wrong with one of our stunts. All the same, we would be wise, he said, to test the whole system out on a dummy before Apples entrusted his life to it; and this we did. It worked fine: the problem was heaving a 200-lb dummy out of the plane door!

Several jumps were then made so that we could experiment with different methods of falling and filming. Upside down and flailing, we found a person could, without warning, move up to fifty feet in any direction in a split second, and the rate of fall could vary. For close-up shots, I needed to be able to stay with Apples as he fell, and this was not at all easy. It was hard enough to keep track of where he was, let alone match my fall to his. It took 30 practice jumps before we felt we knew what we were doing.

Falling as a tight ball below Apples, with the camera attached to my helmet, proved fairly useless; all I did was slide away from him. Next I tried holding the camera in my hand, slung just below my palm. This was definitely an improvement − if not for holding the camera steady, certainly for keeping it trained on Apples as he tumbled. We christened this the 'hoover dive' as we could go out holding hands to keep together, then he would flip over into his upside down falling position, and I would 'hoover' the camera around him, trying to keep with him as he fell.

On another jump I gave Apples a camera with the fisheye lens, telling him to aim it at his face and to wear a terrified expression. As it turned out he had great difficulty righting his position after falling and really did get just the gripped look I was after. Once safe on the ground he declared very crossly that he would not be playing that game again!

Putting my mind to details, I thought it would be a particularly effective touch if we could give the impression that as the body fell his duvet jacket caught against a rock, releasing an explosion of feathers. Amid much ribald comment from other skydivers, we tried, in quite a stiff wind, to stuff Apples's pockets full of feathers, so that as I hoovered around him in the sky, he could pull a cord to release them and then jiggle around a bit to make the feathers flurry about him. Travelling in Apples's pocket the feathers were of course falling with him at about 180 mph; released, however, they stopped dead − having practically no mass of their own − and were left behind before any sort of understandable shot could be taken. This particular idea was soon dropped.

Eventually we felt ready to try for the required sequence in Switzerland. By the middle of February I had my film team and the parachutists assembled in Grindelwald and checked when helicopters could be available. It was bound to take several attempts to get the exact shots I wanted, and for some of these it would be nice to have the simultaneous use of two helicopters. We drove to the heliport near Interlaken for discussions with Gunther Amann, the chief pilot and architect of some of the most daring aerial rescues from the Eiger North Face. He had lowered me on to the face the previous year to film Eric climbing and was quite used to my outlandish requirements. He treated it as perfectly normal that I should want to fall down the Eiger, but recommended that we should wait a day or two for the Föhn wind to drop.

February 18 dawned near-perfect. We flew first to the foot of the Eiger to set the barometric instruments on our parachute systems, then to Alpiglen to meet Mandy and my colleague Peter Macpherson, who was bringing up a camera to fix to the outside of the helicopter for filming our exit. We made a practice flight around the North Face and then back south to Alpiglen. From this, we reckoned we would need to jump one minute after passing over the summit to be sure of landing at the bottom of the mountain rather than halfway down the face.

Apples stood on the skid of the Lama helicopter, while I hung on to his snow gaiter. Then we let go and fell away together. Another skydiver, Simon Ward, followed after us with the stills camera. This all seemed to work smoothly, and we tumbled around the sky for some 20 seconds before opening our parachutes and landing without a hitch at Alpiglen. It was far colder than we anticipated, but nevertheless we made three jumps that day.

We came back a week later − on the next good-weather day − so that Apples could try a solo tumble with a camera mounted on his foot. I would also do a solo jump, but with a camera on my head to try and get a looking-down-the-mountain shot. Further out from the face, not to waste the lift, Mandy and Simon would jump, just for the hell of it. Apples sat in the doorway as the helicopter climbed to 400 metres above the summit, where the temperature registered −25°C. We could all feel our ears and noses tingling, and our hands were stiff and dead. As Apples climbed outside and clung on I checked that his camera was switched on. Simon double-checked and then Apples let go. But the camera failed to function at all: it froze solid.

I did several back loops and spins. The Eiger seemed to rear up in the sky for minutes on end, but in reality the drop lasted only 30 seconds, then, once I'd opened my canopy, I soon realized how difficult it is to steer with frozen hands. Mandy was filmed facing away from the Eiger. It was so cold that, when she landed in the snow a couple of hundred yards from me, she sat

32   *overleaf:* The Eiger West Flank − the usual way down. The North Face is completely in shadow.

33   *inset overleaf:* Preparing to fall down the Eiger with camera and parachute

on her parachute and endeavoured to burst into tears. But it was too cold even to cry, and she stomped off, leaving her parachute in the snow. We were all lucky not to have got frostbite.

Eventually we managed to book two helicopters together. The Alouette would go first with Apples and me aboard, and I would film Apples as he went out by poking the camera into his face and tilting it downwards while he fell. Peter Macpherson would get a long shot from the following helicopter, a Lama. This time, as we made our run in over the Mittellegi Ridge opposite the White Spider, Apples backed into the doorway and I crept up to him on my knees. He gave a final look around, checking the position of the Lama somewhere below, counted three, and leapt off backwards into space. I tilted the camera after him and he quickly became a little dot falling, as it seemed, for ever and ever. He then disappeared into a bank of cloud and I crawled back inside the helicopter behind the pilot Amann, who prepared to descend.

All this time I had been sitting on the floor section of the helicopter. I was wearing my parachute but not the helicopter safety harness while I filmed Apples. It was now time to strap in properly – and fortunate for me that I did. As we came through the cloud layer, Amann pointed to Apples who was still a few hundred feet above us, spiralling gently downwards, ready to land. I crept towards the open door to film him landing, and Amann flew in close to let me get a good view. We were 50 feet from the ground when, suddenly, the trapdoor in the floor fell open and I fell out.

As I swung helplessly four feet below, on the end of a taut line from the harness, Amann slammed the helicopter into a hovering position, creating an enormous downdraught of spindrift. Would I be crushed by the helicopter landing on top of me? But no, I was lowered on to tiptoe in the snow, even more lightly than if I had parachuted down, and I unclipped the safety line. The Alouette touched down beside me.

A quick inspection revealed that the retaining bolt in the floor had slid open, or possibly, when it was last closed, some snow had got compressed into it, preventing the bolt from sliding all the way home. Amann declared that such a thing had never happened before. I was lucky to get away with no more injury than a bruised arm, a crushed finger and a wobbly front tooth. A week later we managed to complete our filming without further incident.

Our antics in Switzerland were really parachuting stunts – play-acting – and because of the absorbing need to complete them safely, we were not consciously aware all the time of the implications; it seemed far removed from Harlin crashing to his death. Piecing the film together afterwards in the editing studio, a different set of values came into play. In pure fiction, I think one readily accepts gruesome detail, but here was something that had really happened, and happened to someone many of my friends knew well. One had to consider their feelings, and those of Harlin's relatives. At the same time, we were reliving a part of Eiger history that Harlin himself had invited the world to watch. It was obviously going to be difficult to tread the narrow line between realism and sensationalism.

At once it became clear, watching the rushes, that the view from six feet away of someone falling to his death – even when the audience can be in no doubt that they are watching a simulation – did verge on bad taste. A distant view was less gratuitously intrusive and thus somehow more acceptable. This meant, in the end, that my hard-won 'hoovering' sequences were omitted.

We edited the fall in four different ways, each time trying it out on various people for their reactions. Almost all those who saw it without knowing anything of the story felt they had been hit hard in the solar plexus. We got a satisfying gasp, too, from those who did know what to expect. Some were unable to believe what they were seeing because they could not understand how it had been done. The falling climber was definitely real, he was alive as he fell – that they could see – and the mountain was definitely rushing past. Yet he couldn't have been killed for the film, so what happened? Had they been tricked?

'Well, of course, he opened his parachute and floated down to the valley below.'

34   *below:* Few can describe the feeling of falling 5,000 feet down the Eiger. With camera in hand, Leo films Apples tumbling upside down.

35   *overleaf:* The Fall reconstructed. On watching the film for the first time many people believed they were seeing the real thing.

'Parachute? I didn't see any parachute.'

'It's in his rucksack.'

Some people took a lot of convincing.

Peter Gillman found the reconstruction shattering. To see again that eternally frozen image of Harlin falling, filled him with the same shock and disbelief as it had 17 years before.

My most vehement critic was the late Tim Lewis, editor of *Mountain Magazine*, a close friend of Harlin who believed the whole falling scene should be taken out. It over-dramatized an event already blown out of all proportion and simply propagated the Harlin myth. I confess I was upset by his reaction at the time. Though later I went some way towards agreeing with him and shortened the sequence, I could not agree to take it out altogether. As Eric Jones said in that down-to-earth manner of his I like so much, 'That is exactly what happened! It was a pretty dramatic fall; it was the climax of a pretty dramatic climb; and the fact that the reconstruction is therefore pretty dramatic stuff is hardly surprising.'

Reconstructing pre-war Eiger tragedies gave me nothing like the same qualms, partly because I felt less *personally* involved with the climbers than I did with Harlin. Those events occurred before my time and were always 'history' to me; I assumed, too, there would be few, if any, close relatives around to be hurt by anything I portrayed. But Harlin had left a widow and two children; Harlin's son was now a grown man, also a climber, and built very much on the same lines as his father.

'He might not take very kindly to the idea of you restaging his father's death for entertainment,' Tim pointed out to me.

When the film was finally completed I wrote to John Harlin Jr and told him about it. I did not want him to be taken by surprise, and I was anxious to know what he thought once he had seen it. His friendly reply, when it came some weeks later, did a lot to set my mind at rest.

I was grateful to Tim Lewis for expressing his reservations so honestly. He liked the film as a whole sufficiently to 'voice-over' the part of Heckmair, who could speak little English. In the end you have to settle for what is the best translation of events according to your own conscience, and not allow personal feelings to distort your image of the 'truth' of history, however recent. That the film collected a creditable bag of awards from various international film festivals made me feel that by and large I might just have got the balance right.

36   The Eiger in winter. Brian Molyneux unsure whether he is playing Dougal Haston or Layton Kor.

4 · THE SAD SUMMER OF 1936

Of all the grim tragedies to have been acted out on the Eiger, there is none more pitiful than the death of Toni Kurz. Though it took place back in the summer of 1936, the events are still remembered with shock and sadness, and even today one cannot help *wishing* the end was different, for Kurz died after four nights on the face, having made superhuman efforts to survive. He died within sight of a rescue team, almost within reach. An ice-axe in the upstretched hand of one of the men who had come to save him skimmed only inches from him. It was as near as that. He deserved not to have died, and so very nearly did not.

Toni Kurz was German, from Bavaria, a soldier in an alpine regiment stationed at Bad Reichenhall. With his friend and compatriot, Anderl Hinterstoisser, he set off up the Eiger wall on 18 July 1936, in the company of two young Austrians, Edi Rainer and Willi Angerer. There had been only one serious attempt on the *Eigerwand* before theirs, that of Sedlmayer and Mehringer the previous year. Like them, Kurz and his friends initially made very good progress. Alas, like them too, not one was to come back alive, so it can never be known exactly what happened high on the face. Many people watching through telescopes around the valley caught tantalizing glimpses whenever the mists parted, and it is these sightings, supplemented by informed or imaginative speculation, and by such evidence as could be gleaned from the remains that were afterwards found, that form the ingredients of the story as it has been passed into mountaineering history.

At this distance in time, a reconstruction of the tragedy for my Eiger film would require a measure of licence. I read and re-read the relevant chapters in Heinrich Harrer's excellent book *The White Spider*, but this was written more than twenty years after Kurz's climb. Harrer could speak to the Grindelwald guides and the Munich *Bergwacht* who had tried to rescue Kurz, but there was no first-hand account of Kurz's climb to which he could

37 1936 reconstruction: Chris Noonan, as Toni Kurz, comes to the end of his rope. Bad weather for once was a help.

38 Toni Kurz   39 Anderl Hinterstoisser

turn. Nobody had come back to tell it. For the most part, he had to rely on an assortment of newspaper clippings and stories put out at the time, many of which were highly coloured, and some blatantly censorious.

There were reasons for this.

In the first place, there is the business of the Eiger being a natural arena on a grand scale: with the aid of field-glasses or telescopes human movement can be clearly observed whenever the face is free from cloud. The two deaths in 1935 had alerted the public to the seriousness of a North Wall climb. Regular articles in the press reinforced this, and by the time it was realized that Kurz and his friends were in trouble, rail- and charabanc-loads of sightseers were pouring into Grindelwald and the Scheidegg to see the 'show'. Sickened, the editor of the British *Alpine Journal* condemned both the climbers and 'ghoul-like masses of the proletariat' alike.

To understand why events were so critically reported in the Swiss press – and why these reports, once filtered into the august columns of the *Alpine Journal*, were further coloured by the opinions of its editor, Colonel Strutt – you have only to recall the political situation at the time.

Hitler was already Chancellor of Germany. The Summer Olympics were on the point of starting in Berlin, and these were being manipulated, through the use of propaganda tactics, into an occasion for putting the Third Reich gloriously on show. In Switzerland, as in Britain, there was deep disquiet at the way things were shaping and a consequent distrust of all things German – including climbers. This was only reinforced when a rumour spread that Hitler had offered Olympic medals to the first conquerors of the *Eigerwand*. Besides, there was such a thing as national pride: the Eiger, after all, was a *Swiss* mountain. Swiss mountain guides had represented all that was best in alpinism for more than a century. They were brave, loyal, sturdy and true. British mountaineers in particular had formed close ties with individual guides and accomplished with them many of the finest classic routes. However, the alpine climate was changing. Young men, frequently young unemployed men, were coming to the Alps and the Dolomites and achieving success on routes that had hitherto been dismissed as impossible. They were employing newfangled equipment and new tactics, and were certainly not employing – nor even consulting – the established guides. They were, in effect, challenging the old order. Before long, the struggle was on for the north faces of the Alpine 'giants', and of these, three were coveted more than the rest: the Matterhorn, the Grandes Jorasses and the Eiger. The three last problems, they were called.

Two Munich climbers, Franz and Toni Schmid, secured the Matterhorn's North Face in 1931, whereupon they were hailed as superstars, heroes to their nation, and honoured with Olympic gold medals the following year. It was certainly a tremendous achievement for its time, and it triggered shockwaves of enthusiasm among the top climbers of Europe.

40   Edi Rainer (left) and Willi Angerer (right)

When the following year four Swiss mountaineers made what they called the first ascent of the North Face of the Eiger by climbing the spur which separates the north-east and north-west facets of the great face, in fine style and in only 20 hours, the Swiss were naturally very proud. Colonel Strutt endorsed their efforts:

> We must congratulate our members on a superb expedition, by far the most important of the 1932 season. We might add that it is a source of gratification to us that the North Face of the Eiger, the last important problem in the Bernese Oberland, should have been solved by this unsurpassed all-Swiss party.

Yet here such a short time later, by their efforts on the *Eigerwand* in 1935 and 1936, foreign mountaineers – and it certainly did not help that they were German and Austrian – were implying that the Swiss ascent counted for nothing: the North Spur was not the definitive North Face route. That honour belonged to the more daunting north-west facet, the *Eigerwand*. Moreover, since a route had been forged up the Grandes Jorasses in 1935, the *Eigerwand* was the greatest of the last great routes, the real 'plum'. No wonder the Swiss were miffed and their reports of Eiger activity biased – although to describe this as 'degenerate' and 'perverted into monkey tricks' (as they did) was surely carrying things a bit far!

For several weeks during that summer of 1936 the campsites at Kleine Scheidegg and Alpiglen were occupied by some of the best young climbers of the day, anxious to get to grips with the *Eigerwand*. Besides Kurz and Hinterstoisser, Rainer and Angerer, there were Herbst and Teufel, Stolze and Haas, Zimmermann and Wollenweber. There was even a woman – Loulou Boulaz, a formidable Swiss miss who had already made an ascent of the North Face of the Grandes Jorasses. She was partnered by Raymond Lambert, who in 1952 was to come within a few hundred feet of being the first man to reach the summit of Everest.

Day after day the climbers woke to dripping canvas and the prospect of the vast face plastered in fresh snow and muffled in mist. It seemed as if it would never come into condition. The clatter of stonefalls and avalanches was almost continuous. For such a serious enterprise, the weather was inconceivably bad. Fretful at the inactivity, Herbst and Teufel decided as a training climb to attempt the North Face of the Schneehorn. They succeeded in making the first ascent, but on the descent Teufel slipped, pulling his companion with him. Teufel died and Herbst was badly injured.

Rainer and Angerer reconnoitred the lower section of the Eiger Wall. They were looking for an alternative to the demanding direct line taken by

Sedlmayer and Mehringer the year before – and found it by traversing over to the right and climbing up the First Pillar, then the Shattered Pillar above it, to the foot of the Rote Fluh, a large and prominent red-coloured cliff which is a major landmark on the face. Here they discovered a good bivouac under the cliff, the Wet Cave. But they woke the next morning, soaked through, to find the weather still awful, and a lot of loose, heavy snow over the lower sections of the face; they decided to come back down without establishing how they should proceed further.

Hinterstoisser and Kurz also made a sortie on to the Face, taking the same line as the two Austrians. The snow held well and they, too, reached the bivouac site under the Rote Fluh, reached it in fact far more quickly than they had anticipated. All the same, they decided against reconnoitring further and started back down the same day. Hinterstoisser, following Kurz, trusted his weight to one of the pitons left by Angerer and Rainer. It pulled out and toppled him off into space. Fifteen metres below, Kurz was not belayed: there was no way he could have arrested Hinterstoisser's flight once the rope pulled taut between them. Hinterstoisser hurtled past, falling some 40 metres before bouncing on to a snow ledge. Miraculously he was able to roll over and keep his balance. His catlike agility and quick thinking had saved them both, and he escaped with nothing more serious than a sore knee.

Already it was into the second half of July and still there was no sign of a let-up in the weather. One by one the other parties ran out of time and went home, until only Kurz and Hinterstoisser, and Rainer and Angerer, were left, unwilling yet to abandon hope. Surely the weather had to change some time? There had been one short sunny day, but then the clouds had clamped down and once more it began to drizzle. This meant more snow higher up.

It is often said that these early Eiger contenders came to grief because, based on their experiences on the big rock walls of the Eastern Alps, they treated the Eiger too much as a *rock* wall, ignoring the fact that far more often it was really a snow and ice route. To me, this seems ridiculous. No one could sit for several weeks in front of a mountain, watch the snow continually falling on to it, and not expect it to be almost completely glazed with ice. There are years, it is true, when the rocks of the Eiger are damp, rather than icy, but 1936 clearly was not one of these, and all four men must have been aware of it.

They had with them a quantity of pitons and hammers, but these were all very heavy and limited the amount of food and clothing they could carry as well. Their rucksacks were said to contain 20 rock pegs, 10 ice pegs, 140 metres of rope and some line, 1 lb of bacon, a loaf of black bread, 3 tins of sardines, some tea, sugar and meta fuel. That was all. There is no mention of

41   1935 reconstruction: Max Sedlmayer and Karl Mehringer at Death Bivouac, with
constant avalanches pouring down and making it all almost too realistic

sleeping bags although in some accounts a waterproof sheet is included.
'They left their surplus bivouac equipment in their tent,' it said in one
report; another remarked how cold they must have been 'despite their good
bivouac gear'. It is hard to imagine what their 'good' gear might be and how
on earth they managed to keep warm at night. Certainly they had none of the
waterproof nylon fabrics that we have now, no down-filled duvets, no
fibre-pile jackets. From the photographs their climbing outfits seem pretty
rudimentary – probably just tweeds and gaberdines – they would have been
soaked through in minutes and become extremely heavy. Obviously errors
of judgment were made over what to take, and their rations were pitifully
inadequate.

On the evening of 17 July, a Friday, the weather seemed at last to be
improving. The night was starry and clear. For the four men it was just what
they had been waiting for and they prepared to go at once. Already they had
decided to join forces and climb as a party of four, and their rucksacks had
been standing ready-packed for some time. They were in high spirits as they

made their last-minute preparations, laughing and joking with reporters. Hinterstoisser emptied his camera and stowed the day's photographs away in the spare rucksack he was leaving in the little tent.

'If anything should happen to us,' he told a Swiss journalist, 'then the film is there and you'll know where to find it.'

Rainer and Angerer had earlier offended some people when they had quipped to Swiss newspapermen, 'We have come to climb your Wall for you ... since you won't do it for yourselves!'

They are also said to have remarked – which now seems painfully prophetic – 'We have become so involved with this mountain, that Wall *belongs* to us ... or we to it.'

The climb was dubbed a 'suicidal folly' by many, and the four men accused of cheap advertisement and of debasing mountaineering. Still, I find myself in strong sympathy with the young climbers. Under a barrage of inane questioning it is so easy to toss out retorts which lend themselves to misinterpretation. Taken out of context, such unconsidered remarks can be imbued with whatever meaning a reporter chooses. Surely Mallory's rationale for climbing Everest, 'Because it's there!' was just one such slick or despairing riposte, or maybe even a sarcastic put-down, but that is not how it has been relayed to us over these many years!

What finally gives the lie to any death-wish or unhealthy disregard for personal safety on the part of the four Eiger contenders is their own testimony. As they set off, they are reported to have said, 'Of course we don't want to die. We are still young and still have much to live for. We intend to keep our retreat open at all times. But we do need luck. We appreciate that, and we must bank on having it.'

As we know now, tragically that was the one thing they did not do: they did *not* keep their retreat route open.

To get from the bivouac site at the foot of the Rote Fluh across to the start of the First Icefield, it is necessary to make a *descending* traverse left across smooth intervening slabs. Hinterstoisser, who was probably the most experienced of the four on rock, led the delicate section, tensioning himself on the rope. It seemed comparatively easy and by 9.25 a.m. all four were safely across. Then, without thinking, they cut off their retreat – by withdrawing the rope from the traverse. They were still in the early stages of the climb and it would have seemed foolish to them to part with a rope when they did not know what lay ahead higher up. Retreat, at that stage, was the last thing in their minds. So small a thing, and yet it was the single most important key to the disaster that followed. What they had dismissed, or failed to anticipate, was that without a rope in place it would be virtually impossible to reverse the traverse, climbing upwards across the smooth slabs, especially if they were exhausted.

They were now back close to the 1935 route, but had saved many hours by their deviation. All the same, for the people watching through telescopes, progress from now on seemed interminably slow. There was no doubt that the four were climbing with the utmost caution, securing each other as they went: they were not recklessly forging upward with no thought for the consequences. Everyone was forced to admit that they appeared to be competent mountaineers.

Two hours slowly passed, two very tense hours, before the lead climber reached the place where Sedlmayer and Mehringer were believed to have spent their second night. It was tucked tight under the rock step separating the First Icefield from the Second. Here they wasted five hours fruitlessly trying to climb straight up the rock section. It would not 'go', it was too steep, overhanging in places and very loose. By 4.30 they had decided to abandon this line. Already it was close to evening and they had to decide quickly on somewhere to spend the night. They could be seen struggling up the right-hand side of the snowfield towards the tier of rocks above the Rote Fluh. Around 7 p.m. they huddled under an overhang and settled down for the night.

They had made what seemed like incredible progress, putting more than half the wall behind them in a single day. At this rate they could confidently be expected to push on to the top the next day, or, at worst, the day after that. They passed the night cramped closely together on their little perch. It could not have been at all comfortable, for although the night was clear, it was intensely cold. At first light they stirred and stiffly, painfully, moved on. It was Sunday, but for them no day of rest.

The night before observers had feared that one of the climbers might have been injured by a stone as he came up the Second Icefield. Someone certainly remained motionless there for half an hour or more. The fact that they went on and not back seemed to dispel these worries. Yet they were making only slow headway. Hinterstoisser was leading, towards the left along the upper edge of the snowfield, with Kurz following. Then they were obscured in mist and for all that Sunday, as clouds rolled around the face, nothing was seen. It was imagined hopefully that, before bedding down for a second night, they would reach a point not far below the summit. But when Monday morning came and the watchers got their next glimpse of the men, they were, to everyone's disappointment, much lower, still below the level of Death Bivouac which had been Sedlmayer's and Mehringer's high point.

Kurz and Hinterstoisser led off again, up the Flat Iron, but the others

42   The shadow of the West Flank almost touches Death Bivouac

were slow to follow. Then, after a few hours, the figures could be seen retreating, and a little later all four were counted back in their Sunday night bivouac site. Why had they given up? Were the difficulties too great after all, viewers wondered, or was it indeed that one of the climbers had been injured earlier? As the day progressed it became clear that the latter must have been the case, for one man was always behind the rest, always being assisted by his colleagues. (Much later, when Angerer's body was eventually recovered, he was found to have a severe headwound, wrapped in bandages. This must surely have been sustained on the Saturday.)

That day they continued back down the huge Second Icefield and abseiled with difficulty down the steep cliffs separating it from the First Icefield. Their third night out was spent at or close to the Swallow's Nest. By this time the four men must have been soaked to the skin and very cold, and they still had another 1,800 feet between them and the foot of the face.

On Tuesday 21, the weather was even worse. In the valley it was raining torrentially; on the face this came down as snow. Not only would their clothes have been stiffly frozen, but also the ropes, making them extremely hard to manipulate. With difficulty the four approached the traverse move which should have taken them back across the foot of the Rote Fluh, the section now known as the Hinterstoisser Traverse. This time Hinterstoisser was unable to cross the blank wall. It was coated in ice, and in his exhausted state, without his fixed rope, he could not gain sufficient height to work his way across. After a while he was forced to give up. Thick mist obscured a possible escape line and, believing there to be no alternative, Hinterstoisser began to rope straight down the overhanging cliffs.

Below the Rote Fluh there is a hole in the wall of the mountain known as the *Stollenloch*. Through it, all the unwanted stones and rubble were despatched when the Eiger Railway was being built. Knowing the climbers to be somewhere above him on that Tuesday morning, a railway-ganger working on the line in that section came out of the hole to take a look, hoping to be able to make contact with them. He shouted and yodelled, but received no reply. Down in Alpiglen this was taken as a call for help from the Wall. Towards midday the railway-worker came out of the hole and yelled again. This time the four were about 200 metres above him and he was able to make them hear him. Forming the impression that they were all right and would soon be safely down to where he was, he cleared snow away from the entrance to the hole, left a shovel sticking out to mark the spot, and hurried back inside to make a pot of tea.

But the four did not come down, did not in fact make any further progress at all. Why, we do not know. Perhaps they had run out of pegs and were unable to set up more abseils. When the ganger, growing anxious by this time, came out some while later, he could hear desperate cries coming from above. Immediately he ran inside to telephone for assistance.

His message was picked up by three Wengen guides who were sheltering from the storm at the Eigergletscher Station – Christian and Adolf Rubi and Hans Schlunegger. A special train brought them to the *Stollenloch*, where they climbed out on to the face. They must be praised for their lack of hesitation: the Interlaken authorities had imposed a ban on *all* climbing on the *Eigerwand* and local rescue officials had stated their refusal to go to the aid of anyone in distress on it. The three guides ignored both. They traversed three rope-lengths out on to the face, reaching a spot 100 metres below where Kurz was hanging in a rope sling. Already it was growing dark, and there was really nothing they could do to help him that night. By this time, Kurz was the only one left alive, in a hideous position, tied to the dead bodies of his friends, and continually bombarded by falling stones and

43 Adolf Rubi, one of the guides who tried to rescue Toni Kurz

sluicing water. His cries were growing frantic and they found it heartbreaking to have to leave him and make their way back to the railway entrance. It was far from certain that he could survive another night in the open.

The three guides spent the night in the tunnel and at first light were joined by a colleague, Arnold Glatthard. When they stepped outside they were relieved to hear Toni Kurz still shouting, though he must have spent a fearful night. Leaving Christian Rubi on watch, Schlunegger, Glatthard and Adolf Rubi made their way gingerly across the face, frequently threatened by falling stones, till they came to the band of snow beneath the overhang. From this point Kurz was once more hidden from view although only 45 metres above them. They could hear his plaintive cries, 'Help! Help! Help!'

All the same, he seemed to be in fairly good shape, having survived the night surprisingly well. He was quite lucid as he told them what had happened the previous day. Hinterstoisser had fallen in the morning and plunged all the way to the bottom of the face. Angerer, the one with the head injury, had also slipped. Although his fall was scarcely more than 12 metres, he had been strangled in the coils of the rope, or had frozen to death – at any rate, his body was still hanging below Kurz. Probably as a result of Angerer's fall, Rainer had been jerked on the rope tight up against his belay, crashing him into the rock. Unable to move, he too had frozen to death there.

The guides had no way of getting up to Kurz and begged him to lower down some form of line, on to which they could tie a rope for him to pull up. Kurz was obliged to clamber down, then up, between the two corpses, cutting them free with his axe to retrieve as much rope as possible, and then when he found this to be too short, to unravel the strands to obtain extra length. By tying together all the pieces thus gained, he was able to improvise a line of some 40 metres, but it took him four hours of excruciating effort. He lowered it down. Still it was not long enough. He added a length of his rope sling, making it up to 50 metres, and this time the waiting guides were able to grab hold of the end.

Sometime between 8 and 9 a.m., while this was going on, a great avalanche came down, narrowly missing the guides. Among the snow and rocks there was a falling body. They thought at first it must be Kurz – but no, Toni was still there; it was the body of Angerer that Kurz had cut free with his axe.

For Kurz to abseil down to where the guides were standing, it was obvious from the length of the improvised line he had lowered that he was going to need a good rope of at least 50 metres. This is where another crucial factor in the disaster came into play. The guides sent up a rope of 40 metres only. When they realized it was too short, they were obliged to tie another rope to it. Glatthard recalled afterwards that from where he stood the knot joining the two ropes was hanging down five or six metres above his head and, positioned awkwardly as he was, he could not climb up to reach it. A karabiner and two pegs were also sent up to enable Kurz to set up an abseil.

After what seemed an interminable wait, Kurz appeared in view over the lip of the overhang, inching his way down towards them. He was abseiling in a sit sling and it was a painfully slow process. One arm was completely useless from frostbite, but he held it crooked around the rope for balance, using his good right hand as a brake.

'I felt immediately as he came closer to us through the air that he was no longer one hundred per cent,' Glatthard said afterwards. 'He was already half-dead.'

By now Kurz spoke only in snatches and frequently incoherently. In one of his clearer moments, he looked at Glatthard and started to say, 'Don't I know you?'

Glatthard encouraged him, 'Yes, my name is Arnold – and you are Toni . . .'

'Ah yes. You are there . . .'

His words petered out. By now he had come down as far as the knot in the two ropes. This was the final stage in the tragedy. The knot would not pass through his karabiner. It jammed fast. Kurz had struggled so hard to get this far, had overcome quite staggering odds, and now the accursed knot would not slide through the karabiner! It was all too much! The guides shouted encouragement, but for five minutes Kurz was unable to respond.

'Look, I'll send you up a knife,' Glatthard called up to him. 'You can cut the rope above you. We are all safe here. We won't come off. You cut the rope and you won't fall more than five metres down to us – and we will hold you. Go on! And then you will be safe!'

But it was too late.

'No more, no more,' Kurz moaned, and, finally letting go with his good arm, he tipped over. He did not speak again. Within five minutes he was dead, swinging like an old bundle on his rope, with icicles on his crampons eight inches long. Glatthard said afterwards that it was the saddest day of his life.

'He was such a nice man. Blond. Nice. I was so sorry for him. And it was terrible for us too, you know. To reach him so close and not to be able to bring him down.'

All through the summer I was working in Pontresina with Fred Zinnemann, I had been brooding over the tragic events of 1936 and wondering how to re-enact them on film. The fact that *Five Days One Summer* was set around the same period immersed me all the more in the mood of the time, and of course I watched with great interest to see how Zinnemann was attempting to capture a mid-thirties flavour. Working on the glacier with us was a full Hollywood-style crew of around one hundred people. There were plenty of brains to pick and, as the epic drew to a close, an assortment of props that could be scrounged or salvaged to help my project. For my re-enactment I was going to need a dummy, Kurz was going to need icicles on his crampons, and we could do with loads of cork rocks for the various stonefalls.

Icicles were no problem. The Special Effects people told me how to make them out of clear Perspex held over a flame and drawn into the required shape. They would need to be sanded down to make them crystal-clear, and should be smeared with glycerine to make them glisten while filming.

Two of Zinnemann's dummies were left down a crevasse on the mountainside where they had fallen. I suggested to Eric Jones that we might go back and collect them. Hamish MacInnes had already tried unsuccessfully to retrieve them by dangling out of a helicopter, but it was pretty dangerous and he had given it up as not really justifiable. The day before we were due to leave, Eric went off to try a bit of body-snatching, while I collected up as many cork rocks as I could cram into seven large polythene sacks.

44 *opposite:* Dave 'Cubby' Cuthbertson, as Anderl Hinterstoisser, tensions across the Hinterstoisser Traverse

45 *above:* Watched by Angerer, Rainer and Kurz, Hinterstoisser leads across the traverse named after him

The Special Effects Department had flown six helicopter-nets full of these cork and polystyrene rocks up the mountain. It had taken somebody three months to make and paint them, but having been hurled down upon Sean Connery, they had now served their purpose. It was a pity to waste them. I can vouch for how realistic they were. I had great difficulty picking them out from the real ones!

Alas for Eric, heavy snowfall had completely filled the runnel of ice where one of the dummy bodies had fallen. He spent a whole afternoon digging into the crevasse but uncovered nothing. Perhaps it will come out in the glacier in thirty years or so and give somebody a nasty shock! He decided there would be no use in looking for the other one either; we were not going to be able to have our dummy courtesy of Mr Zee.

The filming over, I enlisted such help as I needed and we left for Grindelwald in two cars — one with all my 'actors' aboard, the other, driven by Peter Macpherson, stuffed full of cork rocks. There we would meet up with Mandy, who had been instructed to come armed with aerosol cans of fake Christmas snow.

Peter was going to play Willi Angerer, and Dave 'Cubby' Cuthbertson had agreed to be Hinterstoisser. Eric, as Edi Rainer, would have to keep his back to the camera so as not to be recognized as the star of the main part of the

46   *above:* Hinterstoisser leads his three friends up the Second Icefield towards Death
       Bivouac
47–49   *opposite above:* Hinterstoisser leading *centre:* Falling rocks strike the unfortunate
       Willi Angerer *below:* Hinterstoisser helps the injured Angerer down

film. For Toni Kurz, I had approached Chris Noonan, a blond and good-
looking young American climber who passably resembled Kurz, and he
agreed to join our venture.

I had noticed that to diffuse image sharpness and give a nostalgic feeling of
'period', Zinnemann had frequently shot with black net over the back of the
camera lens. I decided to do the same, but had unfortunately forgotten to
scrounge some of the black net. A black stocking would have to do instead.
We invaded a little drapery shop in Grindelwald to make the purchase.

'I would like a black stocking please. Ein, bitte.'

'One?'

I tried to explain that really one would be enough and asked to take it
outside, where we held it up to the light and all peered through it.

'Too dark!' we declared. 'Have you got something lighter?'

It was all too much for the young Swiss shop assistant who was by now
giggling helplessly. The older proprietress looked on primly. Peter tried to
explain that it was for a film, but I could see us running into trouble with
what kind of film if we kept going. Just then, Peter spotted the shop's
dressed dummy, and putting his arm around it asked if we might buy this as

well. They weren't anxious to part with it, but told us it had come from a shop outside Interlaken; we could probably get one there for around 600 francs. That seemed a bit steep, especially as we only wanted to push it off the mountain. First we would have a go at making one for ourselves from chicken wire, kapok, and flour-plaster mix bought at the hardware store.

A day later we had our dummy. He was rather big, but, once dressed, made quite a good, rigidly frozen Willi Angerer. Now all we needed was some 1930s' clothing. Our friend Ernst Schudel in the photographer's shop took us to see a neighbour who produced from his cellar two pairs of vintage breeches, three hats, a handknitted pair of socks and two old rucksacks. These were good, but not enough to clothe all four actors. The Tourist Office suggested the Museum, but the Museum was shut. We were then directed to Frau Burgener's small grocer's shop at the end of the village to see her husband who was once a mountain guide. He clearly remembered the events of 1936, having himself gone up to help retrieve Kurz's body. Obviously his climbing clothes would be exactly right. He unearthed three full climbing suits, together with waistcoats (very sensible!), two pairs of nailed boots and an old goatskin rucksack made by his grandfather. He also produced a brown jacket with leather shoulder patches for abseiling, which, with the rucksack, he had worn at the time of the Kurz disaster.

The next day Eric and I went looking for locations and found several places, any one of which would do for the Hinterstoisser Traverse. We were ready to go.

The last thing you can control on the Eiger is the weather, but for the next four days the weather was appalling − in other words, perfect for our purposes. Cloud layers rose up, covering Grindelwald, but leaving the Wetterhorn sticking out proudly. I was intending to use the small overhang at the bottom right-hand side of the North Face for most of the scenes. During one sequence, the clouds closed right in, making the whole bottom part of the Eiger extremely dark and gloomy, which ideally suited the scene of raising the rope, hammer and pitons on Toni Kurz's thin line.

Peter made some superior icicles out of two clear-plastic coathangers. Eye-witnesses had said that on the day Toni Kurz died, there were eight-inch-long icicles on the points of his crampons, and a photograph of the body taken afterwards by Wiggerl Gramminger clearly shows they were of enormous length, but somehow *eight* inches seemed too dramatic for our scene and we settled for one of four inches and several smaller ones. We forgot the glycerine, but managed before setting out to purchase a small

50   *above:* Toni Kurz unravelling the rope with fingers and teeth
51   *below:* The rope finally severs

bottle of brandy at the Kleine Scheidegg bar. It seemed a shocking waste to rip it down our plastic icicles, but it had to be done. Eric, out of shot, positioned himself underneath with his mouth open!

The whole escapade sounds very lighthearted as I tell it now, but we never forgot the seriousness of the incident we were dramatizing. If anything, it brought the tragedy home to us as nothing else could. Thinking about details pointed up aspects in the story that had not struck us before when reading about it. Chris, as our Toni Kurz, had to spend three hours suspended in rope slings, which cut off most of the circulation to his legs. How the real Kurz manage to survive so long, we shall never know, but it does suggest that when the guides first tried to rescue him, and during the night he spent on his own after the deaths of his companions, he could not have been completely suspended on the rope, but must surely have been able to take some of the weight on a ledge. Since he managed to climb down to Angerer, then up to Rainer, to cut through the rope, obviously he could get back on to the rock without too much trouble.

In the reconstruction, I allowed the rescue rope sent up by the guides to be coiled, as this more clearly indicated what was happening. In reality, it probably wasn't. Accounts vary considerably about what was sent up and whether or not it included food. We discovered one of the guides, Adolf Rubi, still living in Grindelwald. He could not even confirm that pitons and a hammer went up to Kurz. The string Kurz had contrived, he said, was only thin, it could never have held any heavy stuff. At all events there was no doubt about there having to be two ropes tied together, as the first one they sent up was not long enough. How different the story might have been if only the guides had had a longer rope with them.

At the time I filmed this part of the story, I had not read Gramminger's account of events. He says that Toni Kurz tied a stone to his unravelled line when he let it down to the guides. Kurz, we know, had at least one hand frozen into immobility. Indeed, Rubi told us Kurz's fingers were swollen 'as thick as an arm'. Even had they been able to rescue him, he said, Kurz would have lost his arm, finished as a cripple. It was astonishing that he managed to unravel the rope at all, as badly handicapped as that, and suspended from a belay. I was convinced he could never have selected a suitable stone and tied it to his line in that state. A small and probably irrelevant detail, but interesting.

Our jammed knot worked all too well. But on our set 'Toni Kurz' was close enough for us to throw him some modern prussik slings to relieve the

52   The frozen body of Angerer falls past Toni Kurz into the mist

tension. Our 'Toni Kurz' was also well fed, fit, and had slept comfortably the night before. He was an experienced climber who knew what he was doing. All the same, he found it impossible to bypass the knot jammed in the karabiner. Even using two hands he could not do it. Without extra slings, Toni Kurz had been doomed from the moment the two ropes were knotted together.

When it came to filming Kurz actually dying, we stopped for a discussion about how best to handle it. As we found when we came to do the Harlin reconstruction, you cannot fake a death – even one as long ago as this – without feeling uneasy. It was not difficult to enter into the spirit of the rest of the action, distanced as we were from the actual events, but when someone was required to die it brought us up short. In his book *The White Spider* Harrer said that at the end Kurz, his face purple with frostbite, had said quite clearly, 'I'm finished!' then tipped *forward*, swinging gently. Rubi told a similar story.

'He fell together,' he said. 'His body went from the hips and his head went down to the crampons.'

Glatthard, however, was adamant that Kurz let go with his 'above arm' and fell *backwards* over –

and then of course died in, I think, five minutes. He didn't repeat any more. Perhaps you saw pictures of him hanging on that rope – backwards, his head close to his crampons

I had not seen the photographs at that time and did not until after our filming was over. Would Toni fall *backwards* at the moment of death, I wondered? In reality it seemed unlikely; they might do that in Hollywood, but I felt sure that in my film it would look wrong. It was a dramatic enough moment without that extra gesture. So I shot the scene with Kurz collapsing forwards. Afterwards, Gramminger gave us his photograph of the real Kurz, hanging dead on the rope. It is horrific, and it creates an awful impression, but that is what it is, an impression. You cannot really make out which way the body is hanging, and in a way it is of no consequence. Poor Kurz died. At the very moment, Rubi told us, when they felt that at last they could take him down, he died.

53 The original picture of the tragedy
54 *inset:* Just before the end of the reconstruction: Kurz with the enormous icicles dangling from his crampons

5 • HECKMAIR AND HARRER

During the winter I spent in Grindelwald to film Harlin's climb and fall, I also shot interviews with Anderl Heckmair and Heinrich Harrer, the two survivors from the first ascent of the North Face of the Eiger in 1938. A Swiss chalet just outside the village had been placed at the disposal of me and my crew, and I invited Heckmair and his wife to spend a week with us there. Harrer was already in Grindelwald on a skiing holiday, but he was sleeping up at the Eigergletscher Hotel above Kleine Scheidegg as altitude training for a trip he was about to make to Tibet. I wanted to film the two men with the *Eigerwand* as a backdrop and had selected the Männlichen plateau as the best location to provide this. On the appointed morning, a gloriously sunny and sparkling day, the Heckmairs took the cable car up to the little ski-resort along with the film crew. It had been arranged that Harrer would ski round the head of the valley and meet us there, at the top of the ski-lift.

The Heckmairs proved delightful company. Anderl was a craggy hobgoblin of a man in his early seventies, a good deal older than Trudi, his wife, who was a most vivacious lady. The pair of them had the energy and enthusiasm of children and throughout their stay, would get up early each morning to go exploring on skis. Anderl spoke no English, though I suspect he understood more than he let on. Trudi acted as interpreter. There would often be long delays between her conveying to him what we were saying and Anderl's eventual reply, periods during which they held some animated discussion of their own, punctuated as often as not with conspiratorial laughter. Most evenings we all went into the village for a meal, and I remember those occasions as among the jolliest and most relaxed I have ever spent. The Heckmairs seemed to know everyone and they loved to reminisce. It was an education in European climbing history wrapped in the most entertaining gossip.

Harrer, when we met him, was charming, too, but more formal. Whereas

55 The men who first climbed the Eiger in 1936, Heinrich Harrer (left) and
Anderl Heckmair (right)

56   Eric Jones, Anderl and Trudi Heckmair, Heinrich Harrer, and Leo

Heckmair is known and respected in the mountaineering world but scarcely recognized beyond it, Harrer's fame (for the seven years he spent in Tibet before the Chinese invasion) makes it hard for him to unbend with strangers and he is always conscious of his celebrity. We spent less time with him and never really penetrated his polite reserve.

I was perhaps over-anxious that with these two grand old men talking in front of *their* mountain everything should be done properly. I could not afford to bungle the opportunity. Erring on the side of caution, I repeated every take several times. They squatted on a pair of camera boxes in the snow so as to be framed exactly where I wanted in front of the North Wall, and it grew decidedly chilly when our slope was out of the sun. Both veterans seemed remarkably patient. Later, in the evening, Trudi and Anderl translated the tapes. Suddenly they both collapsed in fits of giggles: the ever so correct Harrer, not realizing his microphone was still on, had said testily, 'All film directors are the same. No sooner have they said, "Fine! Fine! Well done, that's just what we want," than they are urging the actors to take up positions to do it again!'

Harrer had been the youngest of the four to climb the Eiger in 1938, a geography student at Graz University. He completed the last paper of his finals on the morning of 9 July before climbing on to his motor cycle and speeding off for Grindelwald. His partner, Fritz Kasparek, was a young ski champion from Vienna, tall, strong and fit, and well-known for his rock ascents in the Eastern Alps. The only person to be let into the secret that they were planning an attempt on the Eiger was Harrer's future mother-in-law, Frau Wegener. As the widow of a polar explorer, she fully understood the lure of adventure and did nothing to dissuade them from so ambitious a project. There was no intention then, of course, to climb as a foursome with two Germans. Indeed, the Germans were strangers to Harrer and Kasparek right up to the moment they bumped into them a few hours after setting off up the face. Awkward introductions were effected on the mountainside, the two groups eyeing each other warily as rivals, and after a brief discussion about the weather, Heckmair and his partner, Wiggerl Vörg, disappeared back down to the valley believing that a storm was about to break.

57 Wiggerl Vörg

58 Fritz Kasparek

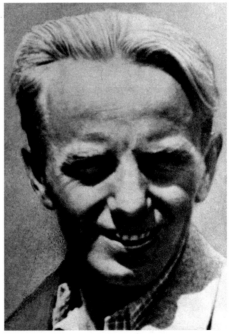

Conditions seemed fair enough to Kasparek and Harrer, however, and they resolved to keep going, although their progress was irritatingly slow because Harrer, in all innocence, had failed to equip himself with crampons. In consequence he and Kasparek were having laboriously to cut steps across the giant icefields.

'The next morning,' Harrer said to my camera, 'when we crossed the big icefields towards Death Bivouac, we saw suddenly two moving figures behind us. They were on the Second Icefield – almost running up it, you would say – and they caught us up at the spot known as the *Bügeleisen*, or Flat Iron.'

It was Heckmair and Vörg again, in fighting fettle but ready to join forces, rather than compete with the two Austrians.

'It was a wonderful team,' Harrer reflected. 'From that moment we never really separated until we reached the summit.'

The symbolic aptness of this linking, coming as it did within weeks of Hitler's Anschluss uniting Germany and Austria, was not lost afterwards on Nazi authorities, who made great capital out of their conquest, claiming it as proof of the invincibility of that union. If the climbers themselves saw any aptness in being a mixed team it could only have been that their success in some way vindicated the agonizing deaths of the two Germans and two Austrians in the Kurz/Hinterstoisser tragedy two years earlier.

Of the four, Heckmair was perhaps the strongest and most experienced, although Vörg had already made one serious attempt on the Eiger the year before. With Matthias Rebitsch he had climbed as far as the Ramp in a hundred hours before being forced back by continued bad weather. These two were the first ever to come back alive from a serious attempt on the face. Heckmair, who had himself spent several weeks at the foot of the Eiger that year observing conditions and laying his own plans, wrote to congratulate Rebitsch on the climb and suggested they combine forces for another attempt the following summer. It was Rebitsch who put him in touch with Vörg when he could not take up the invitation. Heckmair and Vörg met for the first time on some training climbs in the Wilder Kaiser a fortnight before travelling to Grindelwald.

At first sight, Vörg struck Heckmair as an unlikely climber; he was short and plump and enjoyed his comfort. He was almost always relaxed, unlike Heckmair, who was wiry in build and strained with nervous energy. The two in fact harmonized perfectly, complementing each other's strengths. It was this, Heckmair readily admits, that proved a critical factor in their success. They had been lucky enough to find a sponsor for the climb and were able to purchase all the very latest ice gear they knew they were going to need — twelve-point crampons, axes and plenty of ice screws — but they did not care for the fuss that went with being Eiger candidates. Instead of advertising their intentions by camping at the foot of the face for all to see, they took modest rooms in Kleine Scheidegg, hiding all their ironware in travelling trunks. This is why their sudden appearance on the face so surprised Harrer and Kasparek, who thought they had sized up all the likely opposition.

Heckmair took over the lead for the rest of the climb. As it was no longer necessary for Harrer to cut steps, they made swift progress. At first the climbing seemed so easy that Heckmair feared the whole thing could turn out to be an anti-climax. Then, once up into the Ice Chimney, it became considerably harder, giving him ample opportunity to prove that his fitness and training were equal to any demands made upon them. They were now on altogether new ground.

The first shared bivouac was made towards the top of the Ramp. It was neither a comfortable nor a very secure spot. During the night Heckmair awoke feeling alarmingly queazy. Some sardines he had eaten at supper were sitting uncomfortably on his stomach. This was no time for sickness. Harrer, disturbed by the slight commotion, brewed him some peppermint tea, which seemed to improve matters, and they all dozed again fitfully until dawn. It had been a cold night and they were glad to get moving again after a hasty breakfast.

The route-finding presented no particular problems. They followed the natural line of the face and were optimistic that they would be able to reach the final snowfield, known as the Spider, and once across it, find a way out up the headwall above. The Spider, everyone agreed, would be the point of no return. If in trouble from there on, it would be more dangerous to try and retreat than to press ahead.

Heckmair said he found the Traverse of the Gods easy, as he did the Spider itself, despite the minor avalanches which raked the ice-slopes all the time. But the weather had begun to deteriorate. Nobody, he thought grimly, could now say they had done the climb in perfect conditions.

'Vörg was weakening a little,' Heckmair told us, 'but when we made our final bivouac he gave me the best position. I was tired and fell asleep immediately, with my head on his back. He had to lean forward all night, but he never complained.'

Maybe Heckmair managed to sleep through the night in relative comfort, but the others found little rest. Harrer and Kasparek were unable even to sit down, their ledge was so narrow. As they stood clipped to a single piton, it snowed without ceasing. With their clothes wet through, they were even more susceptible to the insidious cold, and Vörg spent most of the hours of darkness brewing hot drinks which were passed between them.

Before starting out next morning on the last section of their climb, the four threw down surplus rope and gear in order to lighten their loads. They even threw down some bread and other food, trusting they would meet with no unforeseen delays to make them regret so drastic a measure. Eating was not easy up here; all they wanted was to drink gallons and gallons of liquid.

Heckmair fell, he told us, four times altogether during the climb, and it was in the Exit Cracks that he suffered the worst fall of all. He was climbing above Vörg, using his ice axe and a piton and the twelve-point crampons, when he slipped. The ice piton just skidded out of the hard, blank ice, and his crampons turned over.

He felt himself toppling backwards and, in order to see where he was going, executed an amazing twist in mid-air.

'I caught sight of Vörg below me. He had thrown his hands up in horror and was looking extremely scared. I could not stop myself from crashing down into him, but if I had not turned away from the wall like that, things would have been much worse for both of us – and for the others, too, because we were all on the same rope. As it was, I did a complete head-over-heels and was able to regain my foothold. Otherwise Harrer and Kasparek would have been catapulted off as well.'

Vörg was knocked from his stance, but Heckmair succeeded in grabbing him just in time before he fell, and they scrambled back on to the ledge together. Heckmair quickly hammered in another piton to replace their belay peg which had been ripped out. When Vörg took off his glove, they realized Heckmair's crampons must have gone right through the ball of his hand. Blood was spurting out from both sides. He winced with pain as Heckmair gave the hand a firm squeeze and with relief concluded that no bones were broken.

'Are you going to faint?'

'I – I'm not sure.'

Heckmair bound up the hand with sticking plaster. In the first-aid tin he came across the phial of heart-stimulant drops given to him by an anxious doctor in Grindelwald with instructions not to use them unless the situation became desperate. If only Toni Kurz had had drops like these, she had said, he might not have died. Heckmair shook half the drops into Vörg's mouth and swallowed the other half himself to moisten his palate.

59   *above:* The Hinterstoisser Traverse
60   *below left:* Harrer and Heckmair in the Ramp, 1936
61   *below right:* Starting the Exit Cracks. It was just above here that Heckmair fell onto Vörg's thumb and punctured it with his crampon.

62 The triumphant four, happy but tired. 'One schnitzel after another disappeared.'

'A couple of glucose tablets on top of that,' he chuckled, 'and we were fighting fit again!'

As he set off for another go at the overhang that had been his downfall, he heard Wiggerl say weakly, 'Just please don't fall off again, okay?'

This time there was no mistake, although he had to run out almost all sixty feet of the rope before finding anywhere he could belay. The climbing became easier after that, but there was no let-up in the weather. Avalanches continued to sweep over them and the snow to fall thickly.

'We climbed the final feet to the summit in a blizzard. We could see almost nothing in front of our noses. When I reached the cornice on the summit ridge, I didn't realize I had got there and put my foot right through it. Suddenly I caught sight of the rocks of the South Face swimming below me. What a terrible thing if we had climbed all the way up the North Face only to shoot straight down the other side! But it almost happened.'

Harrer told how in the final stages of the climb they were surprised to hear voices above them. Through snatches in the wind they could distinctly make out their names being called by people on the summit. They guessed it must be a mountain rescue party, worried for their safety. But, as Harrer said, they still believed themselves in good enough shape to get to the top without assistance.

'Keep quiet! Keep quiet! Don't answer!' they had said to each other. The rescue party went back down to Grindelwald and told the press there was

nobody up there. It was all they needed in order to make it to the summit
under their own steam.

When all four stood on the crest of the mountain at last, there was no time
to do more than clasp each other's hands in relief and congratulation, clear
the icicles from their eybrows and head off down again quickly. Harrer and
Kasparek knew the way down the western flank towards Scheidegg, which
was fortunate, for the driving sleet blotted out any landmarks. They had to
struggle into the wind, often wading through damp, porridgy snow, more
than knee-deep in places. They were tiring fast. Heckmair dropped back
into last place. He had done his bit, it was up to the others now to get him
back safely. Many times he flopped down in the snow and let himself be
pulled by the rope on the seat of his pants. Harrer, who had been the anchor
man all the way up, hauling the heavy loads, now moved out in front to scout
the way. On one occasion he led them too far to the left on steepening
ground. Although they realized their mistake in time, it looked as if they
might be forced to spend another night in open bivouac.

As they lost height the storm eased and the wet snow turned to rain. By
the time they had dropped two or three thousand feet they could make out
the buildings of Kleine Scheidegg far below them with what appeared to be a
seething mass of dots all around them. Idly they wondered what was going
on. The thought that it might be a reception party for them did not enter
their minds. Suddenly, a young Swiss boy scrambled up the path towards
them.

'Have you come off the Face?' he asked in surprise when he caught sight of
them. Upon hearing that indeed they had, the boy turned and sped off down
the hill, screeching at the top of his voice, 'They're here! They're alive!
They're here!'

Soon the four were surrounded by friends and well-wishers, all wanting to
shake them by the hand and pat them on the back. A flask of Cognac was
thrust towards Heckmair and he gulped at it gratefully. It seemed as if
everyone had come up to meet them. There were colleagues from Vienna
and Munich, tourists and sightseers, as well as reporters and men of the
Bergwacht, the mountain rescue, who were all clearly relieved not to have to
run out and search for them in such bad weather. Having no money between
them, the four climbers had expected to return to Harrer's and Kasparek's
wet tent; instead they were welcomed into the hotel and shown to rooms
with hot baths and dry clothes. There would be proper meals and soft beds
that night . . . bliss!

Harrer said, 'We had made an excursion into another world and we had
come back. We had learned on the North Face that men are good and the

earth on which we were born is good. And now that earth was welcoming us home.'

In his autobiography, Heckmair recalls how after three days of eating next to nothing on the face (four days for Harrer and Kasparek), they were ravenous. 'One schnitzel after another disappeared before the gaze of our astounded public,' he boasted.

Only when they stepped into their steaming baths to thaw out did they realize their feet had been slightly frostbitten during the long ordeal.

'Wiggerl stripped off first and leapt in, only to shoot out again just as quickly. I didn't realize what was the matter with him until I clambered in myself. My feet stung as though they had been pricked with a thousand needles.'

The only way they could bear it was to sit crossways in the tub with their feet dangling over the edge. That was how they were when the press photographers caught up with them. The papers next morning carried pictures of Heckmair and Vörg sitting side by side in the bath, legs safely out of the hot water.

At a celebratory dinner that evening, the four climbers received the first hint of the wider and more sinister implications of their success. A uniformed official arrived from Bern to deliver a congratulatory oration that was heavily overlain with nationalistic sentiment. A message was delivered to say that Hitler himself wished to meet the conquerors of the North Wall. From that moment, they ceased to be masters of their own destiny. They were, as Heckmair afterwards said, quite simply taken over by the Nazi party.

'Regardless of Swiss neutrality, fully uniformed staff officials from the Sonthofen Ordensburg appeared and swept us off home to the Reich as national heroes. It is easy to see now, many years later, what we should have done. At the time we were stunned by the response to our success and just submitted to the will of others.'

They were fêted, photographed with the Führer, sent on a recuperation cruise along the Scandinavian coast, and enrolled on to the staff of the Sonthofen Ordensburg as mountain guides. For Heckmair it was the first time in his life he had earned a regular salary. A picture book glorifying their achievement was brought out by the authorities, blatantly demonstrating the Third Reich's appetite for vulgar propaganda. For a climbing record, it contained far too many victory photographs, many with swastika armbands well in evidence. Fawning officials were seen dancing attendance on the bemused climbers, who were pictured in staff cars, shaking hands with

63   Pawns in someone else's publicity machine!

Reichsorganisationsleiter, being presented with bouquets. The portrait of them with Hitler was captioned 'The most splendid reward of all'. It is hardly surprising that in the eyes of the world the climbers were marked down as confirmed Nazis along with the rest. It was a slur that both Heckmair and Harrer have had to come to terms with in their own ways.

'Politics just didn't come into it,' Heckmair said. 'The Italians made the same fuss after Riccardo Cassin climbed the Walker Spur, but I believe that Cassin and his friends were like us — interested only in climbing. In a way, the same sort of thing happened to Edmund Hillary when he was honoured by Queen Elizabeth for conquering Everest.'

Vörg did not live to see the end of the war. He died on the Eastern Front on the first day of the Russian campaign. And Fritz Kasparek was killed a few years later while climbing in the Andes. The two who survived readily admit the influence the Eiger made on their subsequent lives. Heckmair, brought up in an orphanage and trained as a landscape gardener, had left Munich during the depression in the early thirties and taken to the hills on his bicycle, living for weeks on end in barns and tents, eating only what he could scrounge off local farmers. It gave him plenty of time to develop the climbing skills that served him so well on the Eiger. For most of the war he served as an instructor in an army school of mountaineering. Afterwards he never did go back to his gardening, but continued as a mountain guide, working principally with young people in the hostel movement and training other ski and mountain guides. Heckmair's fame made it easier for him to travel: he has justly earned a reputation for wisdom and integrity, and is honoured and loved by climbers everywhere.

It was Harrer whose life was most changed by the Eiger climb. All four had hoped their new-found influence would enable them to launch an expedition to Nanga Parbat in the Himalayas, a peak still unclimbed in those days and with a reputation even more deadly than the Eiger. Twenty-eight men had been killed attempting to reach its summit, most of them on Austro-German expeditions. It was small wonder that the German press chose to dub Nanga Parbat the Peak of Destiny. To climb it had become a point of honour among German mountaineers, in much the same way as British climbers felt they had a responsibility to scale Everest.

At first their Nanga Parbat plans seemed to have the full backing of the Führer, but as the weeks wore on it became obvious that support was being withdrawn from the project. In the end another expedition received the go-ahead to undertake a limited reconnaissance of the Diamiri Face of Nanga Parbat during the summer of 1939, and the Eiger foursome were told that only one of them would be permitted to join the group. It was Harrer who went.

The expedition abandoned its attempt at a height of 20,000 feet. And as the climbers made their way home war was declared in Europe. The whole party was interned in India. Harrer was taken to a prisoner of war camp at the hill station of Dehra Dun, where the Survey of India had its head-quarters. In the prison library he avidly studied the literature on Himalayan travel and copied out maps that he thought might be useful. He also set himself to learn Hindustani, Tibetan and Japanese. Thus prepared, he launched a series of prison breaks, and in 1944 finally succeeded in getting away into the Himalayas. It was a particularly bold escape devised by several prisoners, which involved two of them disguising themselves as British officers, the rest blacking up as Indians with turbans and robes. They were pretending to be a barbed-wire working party and carried blueprints and stolen cutting gear. With a salute to the man on guard, they all walked brazenly out of the front gate!

Once clear, Harrer teamed up with Peter Aufschnaiter and made a remarkable journey across the Tibetan plateau to the 'Forbidden City' of Lhasa. Though the pair had experienced little but kindness from ordinary Tibetan families on the way, they were apprehensive about how they would be received in the capital city. They need not have worried. Aufschnaiter worked as an engineer and Harrer became tutor and confidant to Tibet's young ruler, the Dalai Lama.

With the war in Europe over, the two men sent word home that they were safe. In response, Harrer learned that his wife, believing him dead, now loved someone else. He decided against going back. Aufschnaiter, too, had no wish to leave. They remained in Tibet until the Chinese occupation in 1950. Back in Austria once more, Harrer wrote a book about his experiences. *Seven Years in Tibet* was translated into all the major languages to become one of the world's best-sellers. He was made a professor and founded a Tibetan museum in his home town of Graz.

After an attempted uprising against the Chinese in 1959, Harrer's friend the Dalai Lama fled across the mountains to India with a group of his followers and set up a government in exile. Although still revered as the God-King by his people, to this day the Dalai Lama has never returned to Tibet and continues to campaign for some form of Tibetan autonomy that is more than a mere paper designation. Harrer, on the other hand, took advantage of recent travel concessions by the Chinese to return to Tibet and see for himself what changes had come to Lhasa and the surrounding countryside over the last thirty years. Our meeting took place just before he was due to embark on this emotional pilgrimage, and those with curiosity about what he found can read his account in the book he subsequently published under the title *Return to Tibet*.

Our shooting finished, we packed up the film gear and trundled across to the ski-lift café for lunch. The Eiger Wall across the valley was still bathed in sunshine, and a little sightseeing plane was taking tourists for a closer look at its icy precipices. No doubt they were being told the tragic history of the early climbing attempts and how, nearly half a century ago, four brave young men finally succeeded in 'conquering' what had become the most notorious mountain face in the world.

As the film crew engaged in camera talk, two old men at the end of the table – the foxy, raw-boned guide and the dignified silver-haired professor – were lost, heads bowed, in a world of their own, remembering old friends and reliving the adventures of their youth.

6 • WHILLANS THE VILLAIN

At the peak of his fitness, Don Whillans wanted to notch up an ascent of the North Wall of the Eiger. (There had been no British ascent at that time.) Don spent hours studying the face, working out the intricate relationship one pitch bore to another. With Bonington, he rescued Brian Nally from the Second Icefield after an early British attempt had gone disastrously wrong; it gave him the opportunity to test his theory that a direct abseil from near the foot of the Ice Hose would completely avoid the Swallow's Nest section and the tricky Hinterstoisser Traverse. He was right; it saved hours on the descent. If only Hinterstoisser had found this way down, history might have been very different. In 1966, Don was a member of Harlin's Eiger Direct back-up team, but he never did get to climb the face himself. Conditions, whenever he was in a position to do so, were not sufficiently favourable for him to hazard an attempt.

As a mountain man, Don Whillans was wily. He was a survivor. A long career had given him the ability to interpret whispers of wind, dents in snow, to pick up nuances of danger long before there was anything obvious to go on. He instinctively knew if it was a good or a bad risk. This heightened sense of self-preservation was something that he had developed in his youth in the harsh back-streets of Salford, where he grew up; it was a most fortunate counterweight to his love of adventure. He used to talk a lot about common sense, but we all know that common sense is anything but common. Don was one of those who had it in abundance, and it was that which protected him in the mountains.

Don was seventeen when he took up climbing, although by then he had already been wandering in the hills for many years. He was a short lad, slight and spare; notwithstanding that he was deceptively strong, it was his natural aggressiveness that got him up most climbs. It did not take him long to team up with the best climber around at the time, another young man from the

64 The frozen mushrooms of Torre Egger in evening light

65   Don Whillans

Manchester area, Joe Brown. In the early 1950s these two redefined the sport of British rock climbing, inventing jamming holds and pioneering a range of new routes up and down the country that were characterized by their boldness and elegance. By the end of that decade, Don was prowling the Alps, plucking at some of the best routes there before progressing to the really big 'hills' of the world. With Dougal Haston in 1970 he reached the summit of Annapurna by its South Face, which was the first major face route to be climbed in the Himalayas.

His climbing had become more sporadic in recent years, but it still came as a shock to learn in the summer of 1985 that Don Whillans had died suddenly at the tragically early age of 52. We all knew that he gave his body a hard time: he had been overweight for many years and could always be relied upon to outdrink anyone. It was rumoured that a heart condition had prevented him doing his National Service when he was young, but his toughness was legendary. He had an air of indestructibility that led friends to believe he would go on forever.

Whillans was indisputably the most colourful and the most cherished figure in Britain's climbing scene. Other sports have their 'characters' too, and we sometimes hold Don up as a standard against which to describe them. 'He's the caving world's Whillans,' we might say (or the parachuting world's, or what-have-you), and we refer to people as having a Whillansish wit, but really we don't mean it. There is no one, anywhere, who is remotely like Don was. His flat 'at and even flatter Lancashire whine have passed into folklore. Wherever climbers gather, all round the world, Whillans-stories are told – tales of how, confronted by superior might, or treachery, or humbug, Whillans would win the day with a demolishing sock to the jaw, or an even more demolishing one-liner. To be successful, such stories have to be rendered in authentic Whillans tones, and mastering the famous voice has become one of the basic skills of any British climber. It is impossible to say where truth ends and embellishment or fantasy begins in these stories, but it does not matter. They are a tribute to the man, and he was true enough, part of the climbing experience of all of us. He epitomized the small man who, head down, singlehandedly took on the whole world, endured its many knocks, and held his ground.

One of the most famous of all Whillans-stories was brought back by Doug Scott from the European Everest South-West Face Expedition in 1972. This expedition was led by Dr Karl Herrligkoffer of Munich (a controversial figure whom Don quickly nicknamed 'Sterlingscoffer'), and was only 'European' inasmuch as three Britons – Doug, Don and Hamish MacInnes – were allowed to join the otherwise German/Austrian team in anticipation that they could attract extra sponsorship money for the climb. From the outset the Germans and the Brits did not hit it off, and in a final burst of acrimony the British trio were ordered down from the mountain under threat that otherwise the whole expedition would be called off. One of the Germans came into the Base Camp kitchen where Don was drinking a mug of tea and announced with some glee that he had just been listening to the football results on the radio. West Germany had defeated England, 2-nil.

'How about zat?' he needled. 'Ve have beaten you at your national sport!'

There was the briefest of pauses before Don replied, 'Aye lad, but we beat you at yours twice.'

Dennis Gray, who works as General Secretary to the British Mountaineering Council, was one of Don's oldest friends, and he tells a Whillans-story of the time Margaret Thatcher first became leader of the opposition. She was quick to realize that there were certain areas of public life about which she knew very little, and one of these was sport. She decided she had to meet some sports personnel. So she parleyed with the Football Association, the Rugby Union, the cricket people and so on, and eventually a letter came to the office of the British Mountaineering Council inviting a dele-

66 *overleaf:* Storm approaching Poincenot and Fitzroy across the ice cap
67 *following page:* Tolkien's 'Misty Mountains', Fitzroy and Poincenot, from the other side with the Innominata just poking through

gation of climbers to go and meet her. Dennis Gray was unsure what to do about it and consulted his President, a senior civil servant.

'You have to go,' he was told. 'She's going to be the next Prime Minister, and she obviously wants to meet grass-roots climbers. You can't get any more grass-roots than Whillans — so you go, and take Whillans with you!'

'Who's going to pay me bleedin' train fare?' Don wanted to know before committing himself to anything. Dennis assured him he would and they arranged to meet outside the House of Commons at noon. Unfortunately Mrs Thatcher was delayed and they were turned away with instructions to return in three hours' time. Of course they repaired to the pub, where Don put away eight pints and Dennis four. They were both pretty merry by the time they were ushered down lengthy corridors to the opposition leader's private chamber.

As they sat waiting , the room began to fill with aides and secretaries, all middle-aged and very prim women according to Dennis, who even in his fuddled state could not help noticing that all eyes in the room were fixed upon Whillans. He followed their gaze. Whillans was lounging expansively on the sofa with his trousers undone. At any minute the Great Lady would come in, and the tension became absolutely unbearable.

Eventually, one of the women leaned over and hissed, 'Mr Whillans, Mr Whillans . . .'

'Aye?'

'Your flies are undone!'

'Ee, don't take on, lass,' Don replied, 'dead birds never fall out the bleedin' nest!'

The name of Whillans was already a legend when I started climbing in the sixties; many of the routes I aspired to had been put up by him and his mates in the Rock and Ice Club more than a decade before. He was still affectionately known by his Rock and Ice nickname of 'the Villain' and there were cautionary tales in plenty of what happened to people who made the mistake of crossing him. I felt overawed, but later on got to know him quite well. We lived not far from each other in what was then still Lancashire, and he often used to drop in around tea time.

'Nice tea this, Mrs Dickinson,' he would say to my mother, a signal that he wanted a refill. This was Don at his most charming, but he liked sometimes to play the Andy Capp figure, too. I can remember when a group of us were sitting in his living room one day, planning a trip to Patagonia, and Don's wife Audrey brought in mugs of tea all round. (Funny how tea creeps into so

68 Paul Braithwaite climbing through a waterfall high on Torre Egger, with ice falling down from the summit

many of these Whillans-stories.) Don was comfortably overflowing his armchair, his feet on the cat, and we were discussing who else to invite on to the trip, when suddenly he shot bolt upright, spluttering and choking.

'Is there summat wrong with your bloody arm, woman?' he yelled to Audrey, who was by now back in the kitchen. 'This tea's not been stirred!'

The spoon was standing in the mug, and I thought to myself that rather than thinking about adding more fancy climbers to our team, perhaps we ought to consider taking an expedition tea-boy.

Don and I had both been to Patagonia twice before – he to climb the Aiguille Poincenot and the Central Tower of Paine; I for an attempt on Cerro Torre and to cross the Patagonian Ice Cap – and both of us had been impressed with Cerro Torre's closest neighbour, Torre Egger. An unclimbed rock needle, topped with ice, it looked for all the world like a foaming bottle of champagne and seemed to represent the limit of what might be possible. It had not taken much persuasion to induce Don to join an expedition to Torre Egger, but raising the necessary cash was proving difficult.

'You know what we need?' I moaned to him one day. 'We could do with a millionaire!'

'I know a couple – I'll 'ave words,' was Don's reponse, and within days his friend Ian Skipper, a wealthy self-made businessman from Rawtenstall, had come through with all the backing we needed. Doug Scott had always urged me to make a film about Whillans while he was still in his prime, and now at last I was going to be able to do it. It was unfortunate that, for a number of reasons beyond my control, this Patagonia film was not finished off, nor screened for more than ten years! I am only glad Don lived long enough to see it.

We were a strong team: Don, Martin Boysen, Paul Braithwaite, Eric Jones, Mick Coffey, two well-known American climbers, Rick Sylvester and Dan Reid, and me as film-maker. Even so, Torre Egger proved too much for us, though we did manage to make the first ascent of an unclimbed satellite of Fitzroy named (or rather, not named) Innominata. The expedition, however, had its memorable moments. One day, high on Torre Egger, as I was filming Eric and Dan pushing the route ahead and Paul and Martin bringing up supplies, I happened to glance down at the glacier below. I could make out Don, Rick and Mick coming up to the ice cave that was our Camp 1 – Mick in front and Don the last man. Sometime later, when I

69 *opposite:* Paul and Martin Boysen (on the far right) crossing the long traverse
70 *overleaf:* Don Whillans peered into the crevasse where Mick Coffey fell. The blood stains mark Mick's flight.

looked down again, there were only two figures and to my horror I realized that somebody must have fallen into a crevasse. It was Mick. Carrying a heavy load, he had stepped through a snowbridge and fallen head over heels sixty feet down to wedge tightly where the crevasse narrowed. He had no idea how far it went on beneath him, and would have been frightened to move even if he could do so. As often happens when a glacier is regarded as 'safe', the party was not carrying a rope, and to make matters worse poor Mick was only wearing jeans and a T-shirt. Don had been following about 15 feet behind, and that night in the snow cave he told us what happened.

Knowing there were crevasses in the vicinity, Mick was prodding cautiously with his axe when he appeared to trip. Don was just about to say to him, 'Found one, then?' when Mick, with a little cry, went *vroom* and vanished from view. Don went to the edge of the gaping hole he had left behind and peered in. For about forty feet the crevasse went straight down before curving out of sight. There was no sign of Mick.

'I thought, Christ Almighty, he's disappeared into the centre of the earth!' Don shouted into the hole and a rather strangled voice floated back to say that somebody would probably have to come down as Mick was jammed upside down!

To himself, Don said, 'Christ, that's a bugger,' but he shouted encouragement, 'Okay, don't worry. I'll dash up to the cave and get a rope. We'll soon have you out.'

He was gone about half an hour, in which time Mick was getting very anxious and very, very cold in his icy tomb. It was a great relief, therefore, to see Don's boots finally coming down the crevasse towards him.

In the absence of anywhere else to stand, Don stood on Mick. As Don put it, 'He was fairly well jammed, and didn't look as if he was going anywhere.' Plainly, it was not going to be easy to shift him for he was stuck solidly between the ice walls with one arm pinned uselessly underneath him and packed snow piled high on top of him. However, Don began pushing and pulling, and Mick struggled as best he could. After about twenty minutes of heaving, Mick was returned to a standing position. Immediately that made the situation much less serious, even though Mick was thoroughly chilled by this time and his hands were scraped to pieces.

Don transferred him on to the climbing rope and in about three minutes Mick was hauled out on to the glacier, where he collapsed in a violent

71   *above:* Don lowering himself into Mick's crevasse
72   *below:* Mick recuperating in Base Camp, adding further myth to the Whillans legend
73   *overleaf:* Cerro Torre popping through the cloud, taken from the summit of the
      Innominata. The summit of Torre Egger is hidden. Behind is the Patagonian Ice Cap.

shivering fit from the effects of shock and relief. His frozen hands were in agony, but he was glad to be alive. It had been a close call.

Having accidents happen around him was one of Don's misfortunes. He never got to climb the Eiger because whenever he went there it was either out of condition or he was obliged to rescue somebody off it. On Masherbrum in 1957 he watched, helpless, as Bob Downes died of pulmonary oedema, a high altitude condition that can kill very quickly and quietly, the patient effectively drowning from an accumulation of fluid in the lungs. It was, therefore, a particular sadness to Don that on his last Himalayan expedition, to Broad Peak at the age of 50, he was to witness the death of Pete Thexton from exactly the same complaint.

'I never really felt there was much we could have done to save Bob,' he said afterwards, 'because we were totally ignorant of pulmonary oedema in those days. But I did feel very badly about the fact that in twenty-five years we hadn't actually learnt a bloody thing.' The following year, Don was just setting off for a day's climbing with Bill Peascod, when Bill suffered a heart attack and died.

When Don was at his peak, climbing and lecturing, he had little time for other sports – apart, that is, from motor-cycling. Biking had been part of his growing up, it was something he never relinquished, except during the two years when he was banned from driving. He would go each year to the TT Races, and had three motorbikes in his shed when he died. At most times Don dressed for comfort with little regard for sartorial elegance – he would walk into the Himalayas in a pair of old pyjamas or a floral shirt and hat borrowed from Audrey – but he owned the smartest set of bike-leathers you ever saw, customized to fit sleekly round his portly tum. Bikes apart, though, he was always most scathing if any of us supplemented our climbing with a little skiing or skydiving. 'Dabbling', in his book, meant you became master of nothing. All the same, in his later years he went in for a fair bit of dabbling himself. He took up deep-sea fishing and underwater diving; and on one occasion in America went along to take a look at parachuting. In typical Whillans fashion he hung around the drop zone for a few days quietly sizing up the scene. Before signing up for any courses, he needed to know into whose hands he was going to entrust himself. Once convinced that the odds were acceptable, he opted for an Accelerated Freefall course, which at that time was still very new and only available in Florida.

By pure chance, some while afterwards, I bumped into Rocky Evans, one of the AFF instructors who remembered a small, rather overweight Englishman. Coming from a skydiving background, he had of course never heard of our Don Whillans, and probably thought everyone in England spoke like that. Rocky told me that Don had seemed nervous in the plane on the way up, so to gee him up he had asked which way he would face for landing. Don's 'With me arse to the sea' took him back a bit, but Rocky went on to discuss the body-position he hoped Don would attain in the air.

'How fast will we be falling?' Don wanted to know.

'We don't like to call it falling, Don,' Rocky corrected him. 'We prefer to think of it as flying.'

'Call it what yer like, but I'll be flying like a falling safe!'

Of course Rocky and his fellow AFF instructors had noticed Don's rotund proportions and put on their tightest jumpsuits for the occasion. They were going to have to work hard at keeping an equal speed with Don as gravity sucked him downwards. However, he appeared to enjoy his jumps, even if they lasted less time than most.

The last time I saw Don was when I interviewed him for my Eiger film. He had been closely involved with John Harlin's Direct climb and I wanted him to talk about the accident. We filmed on a lovely sunny day at Tremadog. Don was on top form, pint mug in hand, spinning stories to a willing audience. I was delighted with what I got and once again thought that I really should do a film just about him one day. I was really sorry to say good-bye as we walked to where he had parked his bike. Don kicked the engine into life, climbed aboard and pulled on a pair of glasses.

'I didn't know you wore specs, Don.'

'They're me dad's,' he replied, 'pre-war ones. I've got a pair of me mother's as well.'

'Do they work properly?'

'Well, what I'd really like are some of those that you have for reading close-to.'

'Bifocals?'

'Yup, that's them. But they're very expensive.'

'Can't you get them on the National Health?'

'Mebbe you can. If you're a member.'

And he was gone.

7 · INTO THE DARKNESS

For years I found it hard to understand the appeal of squeezing along underground passages. Several of my climbing friends went caving as well, but the very idea made me feel claustrophobic and whenever they invited me along I always made sure I had something else to do.

As for cave *diving*, that was the stuff of nightmares! It is the sport that starts where normal caving stops. When the way ahead is blocked from floor to ceiling by water, instead of turning around and calling it a day, as any sensible person would, they plunge in with great delight and doggedly fumble forward, refusing to take 'no' for an answer. Impasses like this are just what cave divers live for.

It seemed to me of little consequence that they equip themselves with powerful headlamps to guide them through the murky water when their slightest movement stirs up the silt and reduces visibility to next to nothing. Although, like Ariadne in the maze, they leave a thin lifeline to show themselves the way back, even this is not infallible: there have been horrific instances of lost lines, or lines snagging down narrow crevices so that divers are unable to find the way out. Under such circumstances it does not take long for panic to set in and rob them of all chance of survival. And what if their breathing apparatus were to fail in a flooded passage that had no surface air pockets? What chance would they have then? No! It was definitely not for me. There seemed altogether too many things that could go wrong! I could not imagine anyone doing it for fun, and was not surprised to learn that fewer than fifty people practise the sport seriously in the UK; even around the world the number probably runs into hundreds rather than thousands. It must surely be the most elitist of minority activities.

Not only had I no intention of trying it, I could not see that those 'caverns measureless to man' offered much potential for filming either, if they were so dark. Yet when we were considering what to include in our television series

74 Graham Balcombe and Penelope Powell preparing to explore Wookey in 1935

Pushing the Limits, my partner Peter Macpherson managed to persuade me that we should have one episode on cave diving – if only, he said, because it is so far outside most people's experience. Okay, I conceded, perhaps there was a film to be made about how such a perverse activity had evolved and the crazy people who follow it, but I had one firm proviso: Peter would have to film *all* the underwater sequences. My responsibilities were going to stop at the water's edge.

We decided to make our film in Wookey Hole, the Somerset showcave where cave diving was born just over fifty years ago, and where even today some of its most exciting developments are taking place.

For years, people have known that water disappearing into Swildon's Hole on top of Mendip feeds the infant River Axe which emerges from Wookey Hole some miles away at the foot of the hill. This is easily proved by putting fluorescent dye into the water. The dream of cavers is to discover a passable underground link between Swildon's and Wookey. Divers have pushed hard from both ends, they have found more dry and flooded chambers than were ever dreamed possible, yet there is still over a mile between the last points of exploration in the two cave systems. A story is told of how a small terrier once ran into Wookey Hole and when he failed to return was given up for dead. Some weeks later a stray dog was found wandering near the village of Priddy on the top of the hill, muddy and emaciated and with almost no hair! If the tale is true, this poor creature presumably made the underground connection. It would be marvellous, I thought, if we could too. Now, *that* would make a good film.

The father of cave diving is a man called Graham Balcombe, who is now in his seventies and living in Hertfordshire. We invited him to come back to Wookey and let us film him describing his pioneering experiences. The programme would also feature a modern cave diver, Martyn Farr, making a new push into the far recesses of the system, in the hope of finding a way through to Swildon's. Thus we planned to encompass the whole history of the sport.

At first, Balcombe was hesitant; he had no great wish to be a film star. Cave diving belonged to his past, he said, and life held other interests now. Besides, so many of his friends were dead. He wasn't sure he wanted to go back and rake over all the old memories, but as we sat in the sun in his back garden talking about those early days, he gradually warmed to the idea, and by the time we left he seemed as enthusiastic as the rest of us.

As a young man, Balcombe lived near the Lake District and became a very good rock climber. One Christmas, he and his close friend Jack Sheppard were camping at Seatoller when they met up with some potholers who invited them to go on what was euphemistically called a beginner's trip.

'It was severe all the same,' Balcombe recalled, proudly. Soon he and Sheppard were going out regularly with their new friends. 'These were tough guys, tigers, the hard men in Yorkshire at that time,' he chuckled. 'Or at least, one of the groups of hard men. There were others . . . but we kidded ourselves we were the hardest!'

Balcombe was a telephone engineer. In the early thirties he was posted to the West Country to set up new radio stations at Burnham and Portishead. It did not take him long to discover there was caving there too, and he paid a visit to Swildon's Hole. The known cave was about 2,000 feet long and sometimes quite constricted. Its main feature was a gushing waterfall pitch that froze you to the bone. The passage ended in a pool 400 vertical feet below the surface – directly beneath Priddy church, as Balcombe was later to discover.

'Surely the cave went on beyond the pool? That was the challenge: what could we do about it?'

The first thing he did was to design a primitive breathing apparatus. It comprised inlet and outlet valves, a nose clip – and 40 feet of garden hose! The theory was that you should breathe through the hose, and exhale into the water. Balcombe had to admit there was a major flaw in the principle: you could only go six inches underwater because it proved such a terrible effort to inhale as the water pressure increased! He was lucky not to black out while they were testing it. Later, Sheppard, who unwisely tried to pass Swildon's sump using it, lost the breathing tube under the water and in the constricted space had extreme difficulty fighting his way back to the surface.

'I was a fool! I didn't use my technical knowledge to assess the equipment.' Such a rueful admission was tempered by the knowledge that he was in good company. Leonardo da Vinci, Balcombe reminded us, had made the same sort of silly mistake – 500 years ago!

Impatient for action, Balcombe had another idea. Why not 'blow the lid off it'? Several times he and his friends packed explosives into the roof in an attempt to blast a way through. The biggest of these home-made bombs, a twenty-pounder, rocked the little church on Priddy Green, right in the middle of evensong. The pews rattled and the bell began to toll.

It was a story which Balcombe took obvious delight in telling. 'Up went the hassocks! The congregation must have thought it was the crack of doom.'

For all the commotion, though, when he and three companions went

75 *overleaf:* Swildon's Hole is everybody's idea of what a cave should be: cold, wet and horrible! Converts would not agree.

down the following week to inspect the damage, all they could see was a new hairline crack in the cave roof.

'Someone applied a jemmy,' he told us. 'Whooosh! The whole block, all twenty tons of it, came down. Straight across our knees. Lights and everything went out. We were scared stiff, in utter darkness, each on his own, not knowing whether the others had survived. Eventually somebody said, "Are you there? Are you all right?" and we found we were all okay. But we were shaken.'

Explosives did not seem to be the way forward. Balcombe and Sheppard thought again and produced a more elaborate breathing apparatus, this time operated by a stirrup pump. As the diver went underwater, so someone on the bank was to pump in rhythm with his breathing. Using this, Sheppard was finally able to pass the ten-foot sump and open up the next section of Swildon's. Meanwhile, the team was also pushing ahead in Wookey Hole. A couple of sets of naval diving dress were borrowed — metal helmets, lead boots and long air tubes — for a major attempt to pass beyond Wookey's Chamber 3, which in those days was the limit of both show caves and exploration.

The guinea-pig chosen to accompany Balcombe on the day of the big push was a young woman, Penelope Powell, known within their group as 'Mossy'. She has vividly described the world of 'saturating greenness' that met them as they slipped under the water and bottom-walked their way through to Chamber 7.

'Imagine a green jelly,' she wrote, 'where even the shadows cast by the pale green boulders are green, but of a deeper hue; as we advanced, light green mud rose knee high and then fell softly and gently into the profound greenness behind.'

Bottom-walking, of course, has its limitations. You have always to be attached to base by the umbilical cord of your air-supply. Self-contained apparatus was what the explorers needed, but this was not developed until the Second World War. Even then, closed-circuit systems had many disadvantages and it was only when Jacques Cousteau invented the aqualung that real advances in cave diving could be made. That is what makes the efforts of Balcombe and his friends back in the mid-thirties so impressive.

In Wookey now, tourists are taken as far as Chamber 9, and beyond that divers have discovered another sixteen chambers. Martyn Farr, a young

76 *above*: Swildon's, approaching Sump 2. A good place to test one's sanity.
77 *below:* The water and ceiling meet and further progress is halted, unless you are prepared to dip under

Welshman, had been involved in much of this recent exploration and, at the time we were making our film, he was keen to lead a new team of experienced divers through Wookey's dry and flooded passageways to a point close to the existing depth record (a record set by himself five years before). There they would remain in support in the final air chamber of the known system, Chamber 25, while Martyn continued alone down a flooded vertical shaft into the unknown. The hope was that before too long the plunging shaft might swing back upwards and lead him into another chamber, closer to the end of the Swildon's system. There would be problems transporting in sufficient oxygen to make such a deep dive so far underground, and very complicated decompression procedures would have to be observed before coming out again, if an attack of the bends was to be avoided. It is relatively easy to work out the decompression required for a single long dive – such as Martyn had made in the Blue Holes of the Bahamas not long before – but at Wookey we were dealing with repetitive dives. Before Martyn reached the unknown section, he would already have made four dives in excess of 65 feet. It required a formidable calculation, even given Admiralty Decompression Tables.

In the weeks leading up to the big dive, Martyn's team stockpiled cylinders and stores deep in the cave. Peter and I, meanwhile, raced around for waterproof housing for our cameras, and designed lightpacks powered with the latest lithium batteries to give us as much light as possible to work with down there.

Everything went smoothly and, according to plan, the final push was made on Saturday 30 October. We had already been filming in the cave for most of the preceding week, and Graham Balcombe had given us a marvellous interview in Chamber 3 at the spot from which he and Sheppard and their friends had launched so many exploratory probes in the early years. Now a man-made tunnel conducts sight-seers directly from Chamber 3 into Chamber 9, so that it is possible to cover in a few moments a distance that took Balcombe and his contemporaries many years to win. It gave him a strange feeling, he said, knowing that he was responsible for letting all these tourists see the wonderful sights of Wookey.

The journey through from Chamber 9 to 25 took Martyn and his team six hours and made them wish they had a much larger support party with them. In his final solo bid, Martyn was able to force himself 50 feet beyond his previous record, but the shaft was still descending and filled with silt. Worse, it was narrowing all the time. At that point, wisely, he called it a day.

78   *above:* The attractions of cave diving are largely misunderstood
79   *below:* Lose the line and you lose your mind

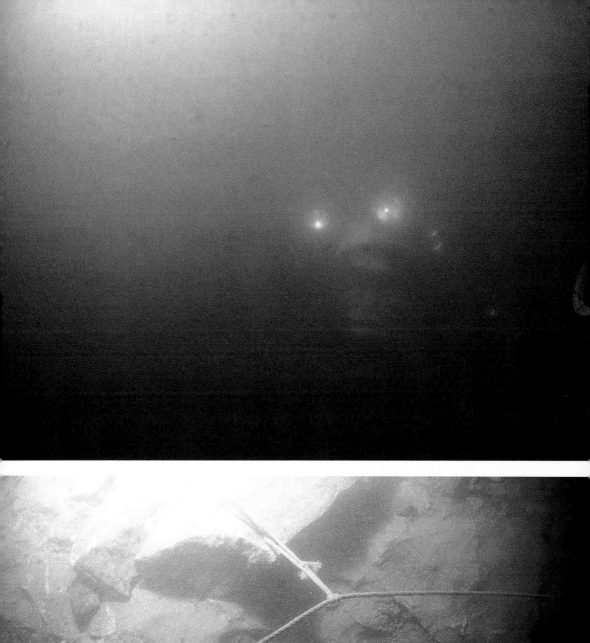

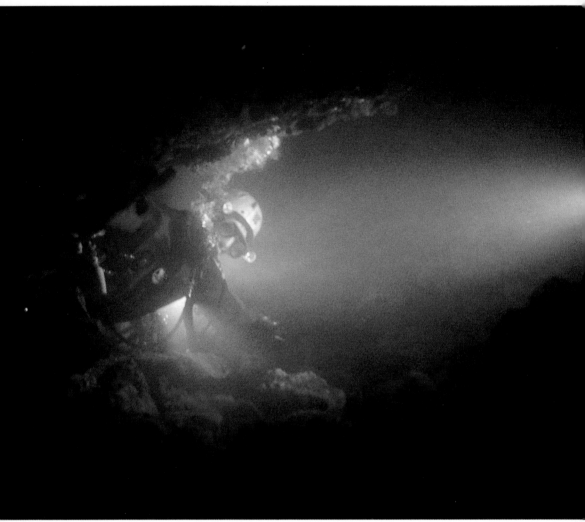

80   Rob Parker in Wookey Hole

To have gone further would have meant digging away at the silt, which was too hard a task so far from his last base, and in any case Martyn was by then at a depth of 200 feet, the limit laid down by his decompression tables. He had gone as far as the current technology would allow.

The team spent that night in their damp cavern a mile underground, from where they worked their way slowly back the next day. They emerged out of the pool in Chamber 9 in the early afternoon, to the glare of our camera lights and a tray of champagne from the manager of the show cave. It had been a magnificent effort even if it had failed to yield the hoped-for missing link.

All that now remained was to retrieve our gear. From a filming point of view, the expedition had been disappointing because the major excitement was enacted beyond where we could follow it. Peter had only been able to accompany the divers for the first part of their inward journey. I had seen nothing that encouraged me to change my ideas about going into caves or making cave-diving films. In fact, throughout the shoot I had grown increasingly miserable and irritable and was relieved that it was all over. I left the others to get on with clearing the equipment and went out for some fresh air.

My car, a silver BMW, was parked near the top of the sloping car park at the cave entrance. At the bottom was a public lavatory. I had just gone into the Gents when I heard a loud crash behind me. Dashing out, I was greeted by what can only be described as a carnage of cars, and my own car was no longer parked up there between Mandy's and Peter's, where it had been a few moments ago. A very shaken and white-faced car park attendant told me what had happened although it was clear he still had difficulty believing it. He had been quietly sweeping up when he noticed my car begin to roll backwards down the hill. Gathering speed, it ploughed adroitly between two trees which might have been expected to stop its progress, hit a brick wall (which it demolished) and plunged through the air to land on the roof of a yellow VW Polo. It bounced off that and back on to the ground, still in momentum, picked up a purple MGB on its boot and scrunched this into a third car before coming to rest at the bottom of the hill.

When I raced back to tell the others, they could not believe I had demolished four cars in the few minutes I had been away. My desire to spend a penny had run up a bill for £10,000!

8 • DEEP SUMPS OF SWILDON'S

To say I was relieved to have finished with Wookey after that would be putting it mildly; its cold and damp had penetrated my bones, its Stygian gloom had seeped into my soul. I do not remember enjoying a single minute of the experience. If there were such things as good and bad emanations, then Wookey had proved itself a place of ill omen, at least for me. Nor did its influence wear off straight away. Even after I got home the dog bit the paper-girl, one of the battery packs shorted and started a fire on the living-room carpet, and Mandy, our wedding only weeks away, wondered what she was letting herself in for and went home to think things over.

Soon after, of course, as they do, things picked up again. Mandy and I were duly and happily married, we travelled around the world finishing off the rest of the television film series, and it was a long time before I thought about caves or cave diving again. Even then it only happened because Rob Palmer, who had been one of the support divers on Martyn's Wookey push, was planning to make a BBC wildlife film in the Blue Holes of the Bahamas and was looking for a surface-cameraman. He came to see me and the prospect of a few weeks in the sun was very appealing. It certainly seemed far removed from dank cold caves, as I knew them – or expeditions either, for that matter. One tends to think of expeditions as being frigid affairs in the snow and ice of some distant mountain or polar waste, not splashing about in blue lagoons on tropic isles. There would be the draw-backs of mosquitoes, Rob warned me, and *no-see-ums*, little sandflies that bit incessantly, but they didn't seem more than I could handle. I leapt at the chance. All in all, it proved a most fortuitous decision.

This was to be Rob Palmer's third trip to the Blue Holes, a series of sunken caves scattered throughout the creeks and bays of the islands that make up Grand Bahama. Viewed from the air, it is easy to see why they are so named, the indigo waters of their entrances stud the ocean floor like giant

81 Divers caught in a shaft of light in the entrance to Lothlorien

plugholes. The expedition members included Rob Parker, who was also on our Wookey trip, and another young British diver, Julian Walker, as well as marine scientists Sarah Cunliffe and Lucy Heath. The plan was to explore various systems in the Zodiac Caverns complex, some of which had been discovered only recently. Peter Scoones, a specialist underwater cameraman would accompany the divers into the holes with his girlfriend Georgie Douwma as camera assistant.

Aqualung diving was not something I had ever tried seriously, in or out of caves. I once signed up for an introductory lesson in Sydney Harbour, but a shark put in an appearance and the whole thing had to be called off. I had not persisted. This lack of experience seemed no great handicap if my job was surface filming, or so I thought, but it became obvious after a week spent sitting around in a mangrove swamp, waiting for intrepid explorers to re-emerge from one Blue Hole or another, that if I didn't get myself underwater fast I was not going to see very much and would miss out on all the excitement.

Rob Parker and Julian Walker agreed to take me into Virgo, one of the new systems they had been charting 600 feet horizontally underground. All these Blue Holes were once land caves. At some stage in the distant past, the sea level was much lower than it is now. During this time, when the passages were dry, huge stalactite formations had been precipitated, drip by infinite drip. These were still there now, though of course submerged under 80 feet of ocean. The plan was for Julian to swim ahead and show me the way, while Rob would stick close behind and see that I didn't get into any trouble. (There would be no easy escape to the surface should things go wrong.)

That first trip lasted only half an hour, but it took me into a new dimension. We passed into a magical world, through cathedral galleries lined with crystal organ pipes – some tilted at crazy angles where pieces had fallen off. There is no natural light at all in these caves (although we took in some pretty powerful lights of our own), and all the fish living down there are quite blind; centuries of disuse have done away with any need for eyes. But *I* couldn't see enough, and was immediately caught up with a desire to film and photograph all of it. Peter Scoones had impressed me even before we left home when I watched him prepare his camera equipment for the assignment. Never before had I encountered anyone who was such a perfectionist that he ground his own lenses! Seeing him now in action underwater impressed me still further. I made a mental note that one day,

82   *above:* Rob and Leo in Zodiac in the Bahamas
83   *below:* Rob with Leo about to make his first cave dive into Virgo. The experience was
      not unpleasant.

when the opportunity presented itself, we should work together on a project of our own. Meanwhile, I set about picking up from him all the know-how I could.

To get the best lighting effects Peter had threaded into the caves hundreds of feet of cable linked to a surface generator. This powered three 1,000-watt lamps which flooded the caverns with light, although we still used our portable hand lights to pick out fine detail. Salt water is not a friendly environment for camera equipment. Underwater connectors have a habit of failing on a daily basis and cine cameras, as Peter found, occasionally flood in their protective housings, necessitating a speedy withdrawal to the surface and immediate dunking in fresh water, followed by a complete strip-down.

'Thermoclines', I soon discovered, posed another problem. These are areas where layers of water of different temperatures meet. They tend to distort light beams, making sharp focusing all but impossible. It was almost as if these caves did not want to be discovered!

When we were planning the trip back in Bristol, I had glibly suggested to Richard Brock, BBC producer of the film, that if he wanted a transition shot to take viewers from looking at the Blue Holes from the air, all the way down into one, then parachuting was the answer. I could dive from a plane with my camera right into the entrance, I assured him. He took me at my word, and so one morning I found myself aboard a little *Cessna 172* taking off from Freeport airstrip. Peter Scoones and his camera were aboard to watch me go. Denis Williams, the pilot, flew us in over Manta Hole, and from a height of 2,000 feet we threw down a weighted loo roll to test the wind strength. I could see the entrance to the hole clearly (it was 80 feet across) and positioned downwind of it was our Zodiac inflatable dinghy with Sarah at the helm and Rob Parker and Julian waiting in their diving kit, ready to go. Our 'streamer' landed 600 feet downwind in a mangrove swamp, so we circled round the bay and repositioned ourselves, then, managing a wan smile for Denis, I edged out of the door, feeling like a trussed-up chicken in my parachute harness and lifejacket. (I was taking no chances – you'd be surprised how many parachutists die of drowning when they land in the drink. A floating canopy can very quickly become waterlogged and drag you down like a sea-anchor.) Mandy and Georgie were filming from the shore, and Rob Palmer was already down inside the hole with another camera, waiting.

Five minutes before I made my jump a six-foot tiger shark began swimming in and out of the hole, and Rob was finding it difficult to concentrate on the viewfinder when he felt he should be looking over his

84   The only way to arrive in a Blue Hole. Shark attack is not a normal parachuting hazard.

shoulder to see if he was about to become a tasty snack. He wasn't getting a lot of sympathy from the others who thought, as a moving target, I would be far more vulnerable and in need of protection. I never saw the shark, and only have the word of the boat-crew that it was there at all, but as the story gets told and retold the creature becomes bigger and bigger, hungrier and hungrier, with ever lengthening teeth, so that now I am firmly convinced Rob and I were lucky to escape its salivating jaws! Nevertheless, the jump worked perfectly, I entered the water in exactly the right place, we all got our photographs, clambered safely back into the boat, and within a few moments the surface of the water was as unruffled as ever. There was no sign of a triangular black fin.

When the two Robs supported Martyn Farr on his record dive into Wookey, Rob Parker had been the youngest in the expedition, only 18 years old. Two years on, he was far more self-assured and the veteran of several diving

expeditions. Though a carpenter by trade, cave diving was his vocation, and Wookey continued to exercise a fascination over him. He was determined to make a record attempt of his own. There had been a few technological advances since 1982 which made him optimistic of getting further than Martyn had managed to penetrate.

Talking out the long tropical evenings in our A-frame base camp on Grand Bahama gave us plenty of time to dream and plan future projects; considering myself now a cave diver in my own right (on the strength of all my recent experience), I got swept along in the plans too.

Of course it costs money to set up an expedition, any expedition, even one that is 'just down the road'. From Old Sodbury, where I live, Wookey is only 40 miles away. Usually the first large step towards viability is to secure interest in a television film of the event. When we returned home from the Bahamas, I went round with Rob to see various television executives and eventually received an assurance from Ron Evans in Bristol that HTV would happily be associated with any future attempt in Wookey.

When making our first Wookey film it had been my own choice to stay in the safety of Chamber 9 – the furthest chamber accessible to tourists – but this time I did not intend to be left with no footage of the critical phase of the expedition. If this new film was to be significantly better than the last, it wouldn't be enough to let the diving team go off on their own through the many miles of wet and dry passages to their last camp. A camera had to accompany them at least as far as that assault camp in Chamber 24. It posed quite a challenge, but I was determined – if I could – to make it through there with them. If I could persuade Peter Scoones to come at least some of the way with me, between us we should be able to get unique film of what it is like beyond Wookey's show caves in what the tourist leaflet quaintly calls 'the realm of the frogmen'.

The stark truth of the matter was that as yet I scarcely qualified as a young tadpole, let alone a frogman. I remember once speaking to Don Whillans just after he had taken up scuba diving in his mid-forties, knowing that courses, regulations and red tape were way outside his normal philosophy. Without the right diving certificate, however, you were not allowed to fill air-tanks or hire any equipment, never mind embarking on a recognized diving boat. Somehow or other, I guessed, Don had been forced to compromise his principles in the face of overwhelming reality. Not a bit of it!

'I thought you needed to qualify – go on a diving course or something?' I'd asked him.

85 *above:* The underwater world of the Blue Holes
86 *below:* In the crystal grotto of Sagittarius

'I got this mate of mine to buy a compressor,' he said. 'Then we got a couple of tanks . . .'

Things become very hard to 'regulate' when they're done in your own back yard!

Still, I reckoned my position was rather different. If I was to get involved in underwater film-making, I would always need the right bits of paper, so I took advantage, when next I was in the United States, of the chance to go on an American 'Paddy' course down in the Florida Keys. Mandy accompanied me and we both passed fairly easily, in no small part due to the instruction Rob Parker and the others had given us in the Blue Holes. On our fourth ocean dive we saw a glittering shoal of about fifty barracuda, one bright green five-foot-long moray eel, the odd lobster or two, large shoals of brilliant yellow flat-sided fish among which to get lost, and the dreaded stonefish, camouflaged almost invisibly against the coral reef. It was a cameraman's dream.

A few weeks later we went on to meet Bill Stone, an American cave diver and scientist, who was to be a leading member of Rob Parker's Wookey team. Bill is the world authority on mixed-gas diving and since Rob intended to make his new dive on 'Trimix', a cocktail comprising 36% helium, 19.5% oxygen and 44.5% nitrogen, rather than on a normal air mixture with its 76% nitrogen, Bill's experience with this still-experimental formula was going to be vital.

When we met him in Florida, Bill was noticeably unimpressed by the extent of our diving experience and immediately set about teaching us additional techniques, including 'buddy-breathing' (how two people can share the same air supply when one person's fails), and how to find your way in zero visibility – and then the two together. As Mandy and I practised on day-long dives, we soon became quite adept. By the time we returned home I was as ready as I would ever be to face the dark waters of Wookey. This was the moment of truth: had I overcome its jinx?

A far cry from the womb-like warmth of the Floridan springs, the first thing that hits you when immersing in a British cave is the numbing cold. The area above your mask and beneath your hood is especially exposed and it feels as if the initial chilling shock could penetrate your skull. As the wetsuit gradually fills and water seeps next to your skin, there comes a new insidious feeling of overall chill. And then the mud! I slithered and fell several times trying to negotiate the slippery banks. Frogman's flippers were

87 *above:* Sarah Cunliffe picks her way through the delicate stalagmites and stalactites of Sagittarius
88 *below:* Rob swims through the wide hallways of Gemini

no help in this; it was like having two wet plaice attached to your feet.

Rob decided to try me out on the sumps of Swildon's. We went in one moonlit evening after I had spent a busy day in the television studios. We were dressed in wetsuits and helmets, and carried headtorches and cylinders of compressed air. Sliding down the slippery shafts, bobbing under stalactites and shuddering under waterfalls, we made good progress, Rob running on ahead to show me the way. A ladder-pitch down a waterfall brought us into a waist-deep pool. (Well I thought it was waist-deep, until I realized I had landed on my knees!) From there, the tunnel led us further into the hillside, downwards all the way, sometimes taking the course of the river and sometimes going off to the side. Eventually we came to the first sump, only three feet long. Provided you are facing the right direction, I was told, this should present no difficulty: you duck, close your eyes, mouth and nose, and free-dive through.

Rob went first and the reassuring flicker of his light from the other side encouraged me. With only a moment's hesitation I splashed into the icy water. It was like being hit very hard and quite unexpectedly with a brick, but was quickly over. There was Rob grinning a welcome.

The next sump was twenty-five feet long; we stopped to put on weights and adjust the valves on our air cylinders and hobbled to the water's edge. There was a fixed rope running down into the water. Rob again went first and I followed. Having by now schooled myself on all the British cave-diving literature, I was not surprised to find that visibility disappeared to almost zero. You could just see your hand if you held it no more than five inches from your facemask. It was impossible to tell where black walls met black water, and the torchbeam only fractionally reduced the murk by one shade of grey. I followed the rope, hand over hand. Strange how your world can shrink to encompass just this little patch of muddied water, with one hand, one facemask and one foot of rope. The rest of your body and legs could just as well no longer exist, though presumably they follow somewhere in the blackness behind. It was a journey of the mind, and I found I was enjoying the experience. The next sump was longer, but I plunged in eagerly. By submitting myself to these restricted conditions, I was allowing all barriers to perception to be broken down. Sight and movement were mere accessories in a world of such sensory liberation. I had not dared expect to discover what it is that keeps cave divers coming back for more, but this, I now realized, could be part of it. I was able to recognize an addictive impulse when I met one.

All of which was very well – but how can such an idea be translated into film? I wanted this new Wookey programme to convey the essence of what cave diving is about. I soon found it also had an altogether less spiritual essence. The next sump smelt like a sewer. It had been a long, dry summer and the cow dung from the farm above was filtering through almost neat. We couldn't wait to get out of this underground cesspit. The spell was broken and we had come far enough.

In Sump 3, I found for some reason I had tipped over on to my side, probably being slightly buoyant and having the cylinder strapped to my right thigh. As I pulled carefully but firmly on the rope a few inches in front of my mask, I realized I was no longer seeing silted-up water but pure, oozy mud. The harder I pulled, the deeper I went into it; I estimated it to be about ten inches deep. Now I came to where my head would penetrate no further because the ceiling and the mud had fused. The rope disappeared in front of me between the two, yet clearly there was no way forward for me. As my helmet struck rock, the light went out. It may have delivered no more than an eerie, reflected glow, but without it the world was blacker and lonelier then I could ever have imagined. I could not move. I was jammed with my arms pulling me into the apex of rock and mud, but well under the mud. No light, no life. My first thought was simply, 'I am dead!' and as if to back this up, I stopped breathing.

Could life end as simply as that? So abruptly, without pain or any feeling at all?

If, on the other hand, I was still alive, why wasn't I panicking? There was none of that either. There was simply complete acceptance that I had come to the end. This was a trap and I had seen it coming from the moment I became curious about cave diving; it was exactly as the nightmares had predicted.

Life had simply stopped in freeze-frame. There was no sound, no continuation of anything.

After what can have been only a few seconds, but seemed like eternity, I started to breathe again. It was as automatic as stopping had been. Now more normal senses took over and I rationalized that as the ceiling and floor met where I was, I ought to move out to one side, where presumably the rope passed through a wider part of the tunnel. This happened fairly quickly and, apart from a slight squeeze with the cylinder scraping against the ceiling, I managed without difficulty to come up on the other side.

The rest of the return journey held no further surprises; when the darkness was eventually pricked by tiny white stars, I took it to mean we had emerged on the surface. A quick rub down with a towel removed moisture, if not smell, and we repaired to the pub. Even the next day, a hot bath and a hot shower later, there remained about me a lingering odour of cowsheds.

9 • THE BIG PUSH INTO WOOKEY

Rob Parker's 1985 Wookey expedition was a far more elaborate and highly organized affair than our earlier venture. Because the small team then had felt so over-stretched on the long journey in, Rob planned to relieve the pressure this time by employing siege tactics: he would pre-place stores and a final assault camp, very much as one might on a Himalayan expedition. He also intended to take advantage of all the latest developments in equipment and thinking. Cave diving operates at the limits of science and significant breakthroughs can be made only in conjunction with technological advance. For the most part, therefore, we had only theory to go on, little practical experience, and everyone knows that no two theorists can ever agree about what will happen. It was essential to plan meticulously and to check out everything we possibly could.

Air Products agreed to supply twelve large cylinders of Trimix for the final dive. We were also fortunate in that Bill Stone had laid hands on some new prototype lightweight cylinders developed for the American space programme; weight for weight, these were capable of holding three times as much gas as conventional tanks.

One of the major problems inherent in deep diving is that of narcosis – what people used to call 'rapture of the deep'. It occurs as a direct result of breathing nitrogen gas at high partial pressures. The amount required to do damage varies slightly from person to person, though a partial pressure of nitrogen of more than five atmospheres usually spells trouble. The diver feels light-headed, as if he had inhaled laughing gas or drunk too much. The introduction of helium into the compressed air mix, as we intended to do, would reduce the risk of narcosis and allow divers to operate at greater depths, but not without raising other problems. It complicates decompression procedures and can accelerate heat-loss; in situations where intense cold is already a factor this could prove disastrous. Our divers would have to wear extra thermal underwear to combat the effect.

89   Rob Parker (left) and Dr Maurice Cross at Fort Bovisand

90   In Wookey's Chamber 3 with filming lights and underwater cameras. At this stage *both* Pete Scoones and his Arriflex were working.

Most of the limited work that has been done on Trimix diving has taken place in Florida. Dr John Zumrick of the US Navy Experimental Diving Unit there has worked closely with Bill to compile decompression schedules on the known evidence. To build up his own tolerance to deep diving, Rob had made long training dives with Bill in the States. Back in England, we sought assistance from the Diving Disease Centre at Fort Bovisand, where Dr Maurice Cross instructed us on emergency procedures and gave us a crash paramedic course. He also lectured us most severely about the seriousness of our proposed undertaking. Clearly he considered Rob to be misguided, if not mad. His job was to protect divers with science, and he did not care for them venturing beyond the bounds of existing knowledge — even if science was to be the ultimate beneficiary.

'If anything goes seriously wrong down there,' he warned the rest of us, 'there is absolutely nothing you can do to help this man.'

We did our best to assure him that Rob, more than anyone, knew what he was getting into and was a very level-headed, cautious sort of chap. Progress, we said, could not be made unless somebody was prepared to go one stage further than the rest, a point he grudgingly conceded, though he could not resist adding that a lot of that progress had been made direct to the mortuary.

'You've got to realize that what you have here', he told us, 'is the sort of individual who gets his kicks out of making love on a bed of nails. He is not asking for a mattress – that would spoil his fun. All he wants is a tetanus jab.'

Delivered of this bewildering pearl of wisdom, he gave up any attempt to dissuade us and from then on worked flat out to help Rob all he could, inviting him to spend four and a half hours in the Bovisand pressure chamber to see how he reacted to the simulated pressure of a deep dive.

The process of preparation and equipping the cave occupied two months of early summer. Peter Scoones and I made several sorties into the system to plan our photographic campaign. On 10 June we went all the way to Chamber 24 with Rob. The further in we went, the more excited we became about the shots we hoped to get. We would backlight this, get a high-level angle on that. The journey through from Chamber 22 to 23 was delightful. We went around a couple of bends and traversed a 45° downward rock slope into what was, for Wookey, crystal clear water. The level at this time of year was particularly low, so that on the other side we were faced with a steepish scramble up a mud bank in wetsuit and fins. In times of flood, it is possible to swim to the top of the slope, but now it was a 20-foot crawl through what looked like brown margarine! As I skidded over its slimy surface, everything quickly became caked in mud – mask, hands, knees, fins, diving equipment.

Peter, emerging from the pool behind me, muttered as he removed his mouth-piece, 'Jesus! We must film that.'

'Wait till you've climbed it,' I grumbled.

'What we need is a ladder,' he yelled back.

'I was thinking of cutting some steps with a spade,' Rob said. 'But don't forget, if the water level rises, this passage will not be here at all.'

Whatever we did, it was going to make a marvellous sequence, especially with an uncontrollable slide down the other side. There were two more tiny sumps, one of which did not require breathing apparatus as the water was low enough to wade through keeping our eyes and noses just above the surface.

Peter and I were becoming more enthused by the minute, but lighting was going to be tricky.

Finally we were in Chamber 24. More mud slopes followed and then Rob held his finger to his mouth, beckoning us to stop and listen. From deep within the cave there came a low rumbling.

'Oh my God,' I thought to myself, 'this place is disintegrating!' I was all ready to get the hell out of there, but Rob must have read the expression on my face.

'It's the River Axe,' he explained.

Sure enough, we came to a fast-flowing, clear river which ran through a separate channel to the one we had been following. Where this flood of water comes from in relation to the rest of Wookey, and where it goes, is still an unexplained mystery. The main river was 20 feet below our feet in a deep, narrow ravine, and we bridged across its sides very gingerly, wary of the slippery brown mud. At the end, we jumped down into a canal of clear water and swam against the current, pulling on a hand line, heads firmly above the surface. This clear, fast-flowing water might give us good underwater shots, I noted. It was no surprise that Peter came up with the same suggestion as he joined me.

Rob was delighted. It was more than he had hoped – to be able to get us both through to the end, and that we should be enjoying it so much. Setting up filming was going to be arduous, but I was confident that Peter would be sharing half the load and Rob's merry men would help all they could.

Now we came to a climbing rope hanging from a steep 30-foot buttress, up which we scrambled eagerly to a high-level passageway. Rob pointed out little piles of stalagmite mud, no more than a few inches high and incredibly fragile.

'We must be sure to get a shot of those!' exclaimed Peter.

Rob urged us to be careful not to disturb them. They may be only clay, but they had obviously taken ages to form. Cavers, quite rightly, are very strict about preserving their heritage.

At the far end of Chamber 24 there was a low-roofed, curved cave with a sandy floor which was to be our bed and breakfast domain for five nights during Rob's push. There were ledges and crannies and holes and tunnels everywhere – like something out of Tolkien. If we stood perfectly still, instead of silence, which I had expected, we could hear constant cracks and groans from deep inside Mother Earth. Rob led the way down a gully jammed by a large boulder to the bottom of a sandy bed that sloped gently back into the water.

'This is where I will be kitting up for my final dive.'

There was a nice high-angle viewpoint as well as one at eye-level. No problems about filming here. We could not go all the way through to Chamber 25 as we had left our air supplies behind, but Rob vividly described it as we waded, waist-deep, through a low tunnel into the silent lake, beyond which diving equipment is needed to make the 300-foot trip to that last known chamber. The recce had been a complete success.

Some days later we came in again as far as 22 to do some filming. It proved a long and exhausting day, and by then I was feeling very cold and stiff. An old parachuting injury was playing up, and I glumly contemplated how much I preferred filming in warm conditions. I had given up making climbing films because it was always so cold, and now I seemed to have taken a backward step. Somehow I had used up far too much air coming in and was chided by the divers for not keeping strictly to the 'thirds' rule: one third for in, one third for out, one third for emergency. Another cylinder was found to boost my supplies for the journey back, but it, too, turned out to contain less than was anticipated. Julian Walker, one of the support divers, promised to follow close behind. If, for some reason, I did run out of air, he assured me that we could both buddy-breathe from his set.

In my anxiety to get out, however, I put on a spurt of speed and outdistanced Julian, although I was not aware of it at the time. Still believing him to be close on my tail, I left the line that surfaces in 20, and took hold of the next one for the dive down to the deepest part of the sump, a depth of about 65 feet.

By now, the two cylinders I was carrying at my waist had done their usual trick of riding round to give me one on the front and one on the back, making it awkward to swim. I formed the impression that my breathing was being restricted and looked at the pressure gauge. It was red, which I took to mean I was getting low on air. I reached for the other regulator, as I thought I would change cylinders, but it was somewhere behind me and I could not reach it.

This started a chain reaction of panic. My breathing became more rapid and I became even more firmly convinced I was running out of air. Desperately, I looked around for Julian, but he was by now about three minutes behind me — which if I had been in real trouble would have been two and a half minutes too much.

In my haste to turn around I had momentarily dislodged my mask. Now I was choking and spluttering as well and very, very frightened. Ahead I could see the line, upon which of course I still had a tight hold, giving out to darkness at the end of my pencil-beam of light. I knew I was deep, knew that because I had been swimming quickly and panting I would be making my greatest demand of air, and yet I was running out fast.

If I went back, I might with luck surface at 20 again. Or I might bump into Julian on the way. Or I might die.

If I kept going, it was just possible I could reach the safety of Chamber 9,

91 *overleaf left:* Ian Rolland straddling the River Axe in Wookey's Chamber 24
92 *right:* Traversing along the River Axe towards our camp site

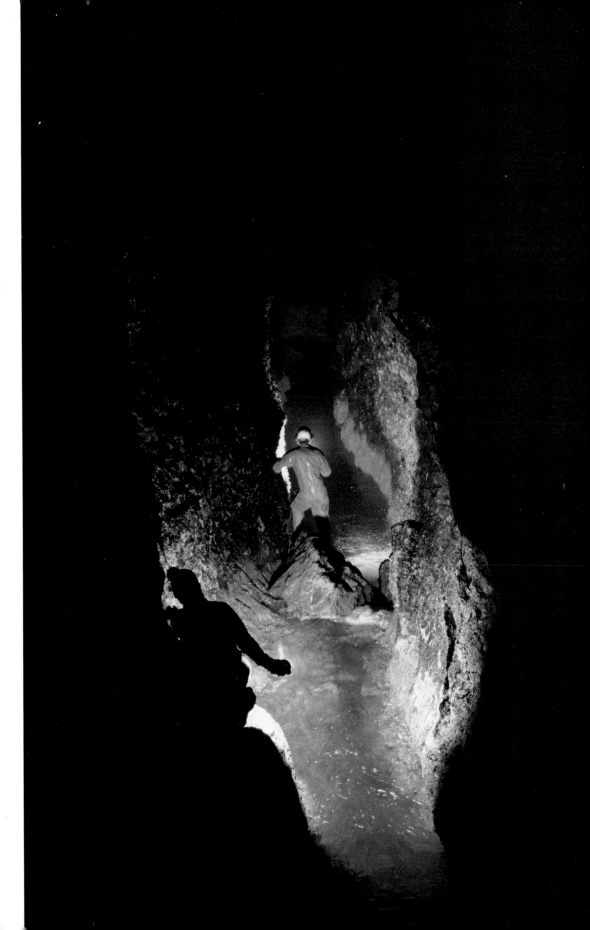

but from the deepest point it was still several minutes' swimming away.

Perhaps it was my imagination but my torches, too, appeared now to be fading; they had been on for three or four hours.

'You fool, you stupid old fool,' I scolded myself bitterly, 'you've blown it this time,' and I kept repeating, 'This is it! This really is it!'

I would keep heading out, but should I make a dash for it, or go slowly to conserve my air? I could not decide which was best.

My life, I knew, was balanced on a pin, and I knew, too, that my mind was not serving the interests of the rest of my body. I had a sudden vision of Mandy and thought with a pang how sad never to see her again. It was a state of mind born out of sheer panic, as I now realize, but then I could feel my mind slipping away and my life with it. I was seeing the world through a port-hole, with me on the outside in infinite blackness.

It was exactly the right way to go about dying, of course, and at some level I must have realized that, for just in the nick of time I took a firm grip of myself and tried to think more positively. Now I could feel the other mouthpiece in my hand, so I pressed the purge button and discovered to my relief that there *was* air in my second cylinder; and there was still some air in the one from which I was breathing, even though it was coming out with some difficulty. I thought, 'There's no point whatever in taking this mouthpiece out and risking further trauma. I will simply hold the purge button and mouthpiece in my other hand, next to my mask, so that the minute there is a problem I can ram it in – and hope there will be enough to get me up to Chamber 9.'

At least I was now ascending, and with a slightly clearer mind. I still could not work out whether to go slowly or fast, but paddled furiously to get it over with. Survivalists might argue that I was a classic disaster waiting to happen, but instinct has always served me well in the past. It's my firm belief that if a meteor is heading in your direction, the best thing to do is to dodge out of the way and ask the questions later. Maybe, this way, I use a disproportionate amount of energy extricating myself from dangerous situations, and maybe it tells later in exhaustion or collapse. Somebody like my friend Eric Jones would be a lot cooler and more analytical at times like this, fatalistic even, but I try and influence fate with action.

It was dark when I surfaced, the tourists had gone home, but to be back in the land of the living was like a gift. How sweet the world was.

When I got home, there was a letter waiting for me. It was from the VAT-man, admonishing me for being late with my tax returns.

93   The high-level passageway leading to the far end of Chamber 24.
      Our bedroom is just off to the right.

Three days later we were filming the mud stalagmites in Chamber 22 when Peter stepped back to adjust the position of one of his lights. Somehow he managed to trip or slip and skidded down a six-foot bank. I thought I heard a crack, there was certainly a sharp intake of breath.

'You okay?'

'Yes, yes,' he said, 'but I think I'll just sit here for a moment.'

Julian came over. We prodded Peter's ankle. 'How does it feel?'

'Bit tender.'

He tried to stand up and discovered that he could barely take his weight upon it. We decided to get him out as soon as we could. There was no problem about abandoning his camera equipment. Nobody was likely to come in and steal it, and the last time this particular cave flooded must have been several million years ago.

Peter found he could scramble, crab-wise. His swelling ankle felt better for being immersed in water. We got out uneventfully and, wriggling out of his wet gear, Peter clambered over the railings to the staff car park. (I had somehow never got round to parking again in the public one where my car had run amok.) We figured that the first thing to do was go for a pint – Peter needed the anaesthetic – after that we could take him to a hospital for a check-up. But not, he urged, before finding something to eat as well: there was a pizza parlour near by. The six of us promptly consumed 24 pizzas! It had been a demanding day.

Eventually, in the hospital emergency unit after Peter had been carefully examined, it was announced that his ankle was broken in three places. He would need a long operation in the morning, involving screws and plates, and was obviously going to be in plaster for at least eight weeks. His further involvement with the film was now reduced to a single scene, shot at his bedside the following day, in which he explained to me the workings of his Arriflex camera, still deep in Wookey Hole.

Quite apart from feeling sorry for him, and responsible in a way for his being in Wookey at all, I was extremely uneasy about filming the rest of the expedition without his help. My worst misgivings were soon realized when I returned to Chamber 24 for the final push to find Peter's Arriflex stubbornly refusing to work and my little back-up N9 awash with two inches of water inside its waterproof housing.

94 *opposite:* Preparing for a deep dive at the far end of Chamber 24
95 *overleaf:* Our camp site, one mile underground, in 'daylight hours'. Everything was packed into 'see-through' black polythene bags for easy sorting.
96 *following page:* Camp site during the hours of darkness, a large polythene bag and soft sand for a bed. Ghosts were not a problem but one drysuit went walkabout during the night.

I was desperate. If I went out for another camera, I would miss all the action. The slow build-up was over. Six of us were camped in our little grotto and Rob was poised ready to go. Almost in tears, I emptied out the water from the N9 and dried it off. With no great optimism I switched it on – and the beautiful little bag of tricks whirred away quite merrily! Obviously this must be one camera that does not require a waterproof housing. I was operational once more, but without the Arriflex had no way of recording synchronized sound. I did the best I could by taping interviews with everyone afterwards.

Rob made his push on our third day in the underground camp. After an early start, he and Julian dived through into Chamber 25, where they were joined by Bill Stone. Designated official cameraman for this section, Bill carried the cine-camera to see what he could get of the actual dive. He and Julian would wait there in 25, in support, but they knew that, as Dr Cross had said, there was little that could be done for Rob in a real emergency this far from the surface.

Loaded with four separate tanks, Trimix for the dive and oxygen for decompression, Rob lowered himself into the water. Visibility was good; he could see about 15 yards in front of him. The others watched as he gradually faded out of sight, then settled down for the long, anxious wait. We were doing the same back in 23. Apart from however long the dive itself took, we all knew Rob was going to need at least two hours' decompression before he could resurface again.

On reaching 150 feet, Rob dumped his first depleted cylinder and continued to Martyn's limit of exploration. Here he tied on his line.

The gravel floor was dipping steeply and he forced his way against the flow of the river, down through the narrow squeeze that had checked Martyn. The full force of the River Axe was now coming straight at him through a gap only 15 inches high, pelting him with its pebble burden. Fighting against it, he came to a roomier section beyond, but before long this too ended in a constriction. Gravel was already slumping in behind him and threatening to cut off his retreat.

'Looking through the onslaught of hail, I could see the passage becoming impossibly tight ten feet further down. I conceded to the cave.'

There is no clue from these terse words, with which he later concluded his official report, just how great was Rob's disappointment in having to make such a concession. The dream of finding Chamber 26 had eluded him and

97   The final lake in Chamber 24 – filming with underwater camera
     the search for Chamber 25 and the still elusive 26

with it collapsed the greater dream of finding a link with Swildon's by this route. If such a link does exist, then it must lie somewhere else and the job of the next explorers will be to investigate all the high-level pocks and alcoves to see if any of them offer promise of a way through.

Thus ended our attempt.

On the face of it, we had done no more than improve Martyn's record by 20 feet. All the same, Rob had achieved what was believed to be the deepest sump-dive ever made in a multi-sump system. And from a technological point of view, the expedition had been a triumph: the Trimix worked well, Rob's head had remained as clear as a bell, enabling him to work at 220 feet without discomfort, and Zumrick's decompression tables were spot on.

As Bill Stone reminded us in my film, success with mixed gas diving marked a new era in cave exploration. It was no fault of our revolutionary methods that the geology of Wookey proved uncooperative. Had the tunnel been bigger, there was no reason why Rob could not have got through to the other side and been able to explore the interior of Mendip. Progress is not always as spectacular as one would wish. It is the slow consolidation of experience that counts, and the experience gained by Rob in Wookey was now available to be put to use in other remote cave systems elsewhere in the world.

98   A lonely vigil as Rob Parker disappeared from chamber 25

10 • THE FOUNTAIN OF YOUTH

For me, one of the highlights of our Wookey adventure was that it had given me the chance of getting better acquainted with the good doctor, Bill Stone. It was a revelation. I had never before encountered anyone who combined intelligence and dedication in quite so formidable a compound. There is no such thing in Bill's world as an insoluble problem: you apply science and you apply logic — in whatever quantities it takes — and ultimately you will be rewarded with the answer. His life over the past few years has been devoted to finding ways to prolong the time a man can live and work underwater. Every major cave dive he undertakes he sees as an opportunity to put his latest theories and inventions to the test, and all the time he is looking ahead to the next evolutionary step.

In Wookey, we were confirming the efficiency of mixed-gas diving, but it still meant a long preparation period while we built up the necessary supplies of gas deep in the system. Even given adequate supplies and a cave working in our favour, the distance we could penetrate would be limited by how much gas could be carried on a single dive. The only way to free a diver to go as far and as long underwater as he wants is to eradicate the need for continually replenishing his air supply. Bill's dream was to build a closed-circuit apparatus that scrubbed out exhaled carbon-dioxide and made the air or gas mixture rebreathable — indefinitely. That way, he hoped, a small self-contained team would one day be able to go into an uncharted system and stay there, exploring, for anything up to six weeks without once coming back to the surface. Borrowing a term from mountaineering, he called this concept 'alpine style' exploration.

Rebreathers are not altogether new: mountaineers have experimented with closed-circuit systems; firemen use them; miners use them in contaminated galleries; spacemen, of course, have to use them whenever they leave their pressurized capsules. Simple sets are already on the market for divers if they are not intending to go to any depth, and Bill knew that the US Navy had a highly sophisticated closed-circuit diving apparatus, the Seal rig. It

was with this that he felt he should be conducting his initial experiments. The manufacturers, when he went to discuss the matter with them, listened tolerantly enough, but said that though they were happy to supply him with a set, it would set him back $30,000. As this was not the sort of money Bill could lay his hands upon easily, he went disconsolately away.

He felt rejected by the only people he considered could help him, but continued to study all available literature on developed systems, including the NASA space suit and, by the time he came over to Wookey, had convinced himself that he could and would have to build his own rebreather. The design was already shaping in his mind.

As soon as he returned home he took the idea to the National Geographic Society, showing slides of tantalizing cave systems where further exploration was blocked until some such technological advance became available. He found it impossible to tell from their faces whether members of the panel regarded him as a nutcase, or (as he believed himself to be) someone on the brink of doing something outrageous but of historical significance. Fortunately, they were won over and wrote him a cheque to begin building his rebreather. It took him just three weeks to spend it, but by then he was on his way, with a small company formed to develop his ideas.

Cave divers can operate with an easy mind only when they know they have some reserve measure to fall back on should part of their system malfunction. It is to give them this sort of confidence that the 'thirds' rule was evolved, ensuring that they always had in hand for emergency as much air as was needed to come in or go out. Wherever possible, the same sort of principle is built into individual components of their breathing apparatus. Bill had designed a special Y-valve and cross-over line that enables a diver to isolate various parts in the system and access either one of his two tanks with a reserve regulator. Such 'redundancy' features, as they are known, are seen as essential to a potentially high-risk activity like cave diving, in the same way as a parachutist would not dream of jumping without having a reserve chute in addition to his main one. Bill told us he intended to build *five* levels of redundancy into his rebreather.

'If something packs up several miles and three weeks inside the cave system,' he explained, 'you are going to need the thing redundant enough to give you all the chances in the world to get out of there. This way, you've got five chances before you are really up the creek.'

99 *opposite:* Dr Bill Stone with his rebreather
100 *overleaf:* Wakulla Springs, Florida; largely unchanged since mastodons roamed the Earth

He had expected to find similar principles of redundancy built into existing rebreathers, and was shocked when his research revealed that none of the systems he studied, including the NASA space suit, had what he would term 'a fully operational redundancy'.

'I felt that there had to be a much better way to make these things safe, so that if anything went wrong you didn't just die. You would turn valves, isolate the problem out of the system, and either head back out – if you felt it was serious – or, ideally, if you had a really backed-up system, continue with your mission.

'Mission safety' (as he called it) was something he was planning to build into his design along with 'system safety'; he wanted to enhance the probability that you completed your mission even if a few things started going wrong in the course of it. To do this meant looking carefully into statistics and probability, and developing equations for mission failure. He finally concluded that it was possible to produce a rebreathing system *sixteen* times safer than any other on the market, part for part.

By the beginning of the following year, Bill had developed the 'architecture' of the design, and was faced with implementing the necessary computer software for the four on-board computers he proposed building into it. With nobody to advise him he had, as he said, the luxury of being able to do things the way he wanted them done. It took eighteen months to produce the 6,000-line programme that incorporated all the checks and balances he insisted upon for monitoring life support, but in the end his rebreather could talk to him, answer his questions, and advise him on choice of decisions to take in any conceivable emergency, as well as supply him with whatever gas he needed for whatever depth at which he was diving. The computers chattered between themselves, with one computer overseeing all the others.

'This was the Grand Solomon of hard transistors, he'd be looking over all the stuff and saying "Okay guys, are you all in sync? You all doin' okay?" and if Number One responds with "No I'm not doin' okay", he says, "Too bad with you. We will average Numbers Two and Three and we will send that information out."'

It was an idea Bill had borrowed from the Space Shuttle programme, where it is used for controlling rocket motors and ailerons when they launch, but so far as he could discover nobody had ever employed anything like it in a diving rig or any other life support system. He could see all sorts of applications for the apparatus when it was fully tested – working out of submarines or underwater habitats, or – and this I soon gathered is where his real interest lies – for spacewalking. Bill's ultimate dream would be to take his rebreather into outer space. He has to have it ready by the time commercial spaceflights become universally available!

It used to be believed that the Fountain of Youth was to be found on an island in the Bahamas. One of those to come in search of it was the Spanish explorer Ponce de León. He made landfall on a lush subtropical coast one beautiful spring morning in 1512 and, from the abundance of its flowers, christened the place Florida. In his heart he believed he had discovered the fabulous island of his quest, but sadly there is no record that Ponce de León ever found the mystical fountain with its life-giving powers. We know now, of course, that Florida is neither an island, as he thought, nor in the Bahamas, but that is not to say it does not offer any number of deep and crystal springs. It is because of these springs that it is so fascinating to cave divers, why so many of the world's greatest divers either come from Florida or make it their home.

In swamplands to the north-west of the state lies an area that the native Seminole Indians used to call Land of Mysterious Waters. It is there, not far from Tallahassee, that the Wakulla River surges from one of the deepest underwater cave systems known to man. Just how far and how deep the network of caves extends beneath the blue maw of the spring entrance nobody knows: access has rarely been granted to divers. It was only with the recent acquisition of Wakulla Park by the State of Florida that permission was given for a single major exploratory expedition. Bill Stone would lead an international team of world-class divers to probe the secrets of this intriguing underwater labyrinth.

It was a challenge to stretch even his powers of innovation. As he explained it to me, when we were discussing plans for filming such a once-in-a-lifetime opportunity, 'Wakulla starts deep, and goes deeper.'

Back in the fifties, the only divers to have been there went 900 feet into the cave. Bill was planning on dives of anything up to a mile in length. It would provide an opportunity to test his prototype rebreather, but of course that would have to be an independent goal of the expedition. The main job of exploration and science would be undertaken by mixed-gas diving, because at least we had the Wookey experience upon which to base that. To cope with the distances involved, Bill planned to use special high-powered 'scooters' which would propel divers further than they could swim under their own power, and also act as transporters for their bulky gas cylinders. This was a weak link in his 'redundancy' policy. If anything went wrong with one of the scooters at the furthest point of exploration, it would be too far to swim back on the amount of gas it was carrying. Divers would need to work in pairs, so that an element of buddy-assistance could be given in any emergency.

The most complicated issue involved with multi-gas exploration at such depths, however, remained that of decompression. Coming up from a deep dive necessitates stopping for specified periods at ten-foot intervals; in Wakulla, you were talking about twenty or more such stops before reaching the surface, around fourteen hours in all! It was a long time to hang about doing nothing but get cold and hungry. Bill set about devising a way to alleviate the whole process and, during the months of preparation, we would receive mystifying bulletins about a proposed underwater 'habitat' or, as he sometimes called it, 'variable depth device'. It was hard to picture exactly what he had in mind, so I waited to be surprised when we eventually made it to Wakulla.

The team that Bill put together was impressive. With an objective that represented the extreme end of what might be possible underground and underwater, it was easy to attract the cream of the world's cave divers. This was their Everest, their trip to the moon, and they all wanted to be in on it. From England there would be Rob Parker and Gavin Newman, and from America, Paul DeLoach, Sheck Exley, Clark Pitcairn, Mary Ellen Eckhoff, Wes Skiles, Brad Pecel and Paul Heinerth – all names I had read about in connection with recent major exploration around the world. Sheck, in particular, had an almost legendary reputation. For more than 15 years he had been a leading diver and it was from him that Bill Stone had acquired most of his initial deep-diving experience. The level of Sheck's commitment to cave diving can be gauged from the fact that he has bought a plot of land in North Florida with its own spring in order to work without restriction towards a 'mile push' underwater. Our physician was Dr Noel Sloan, an anaesthetist from Indianapolis, and the team biologist was Tom Morris. Pete Scoones would again work with me on the filming, with Mandy and Georgie acting as our assistants. Of course, we were not expecting to go as deep as the lead divers, so it was lucky that one of them, Wes, was a very good cameraman. His bold announcement, when I first met him, that there was no way I could make a film about Wakulla without him did not go down well. It was an affront to my professional pride. But over the next few weeks I learned that he was right. Though Wes lacked the sophisticated knowledge and background of conventional film-makers, he had applied the basic rules to his sport and developed a formula that gave him beautiful pictures with

101   The original explorers had one cylinder of air, no wetsuits, no depth gauge, poor
       torches and guessed their decompression times, yet they managed to make the most
       amazing discoveries

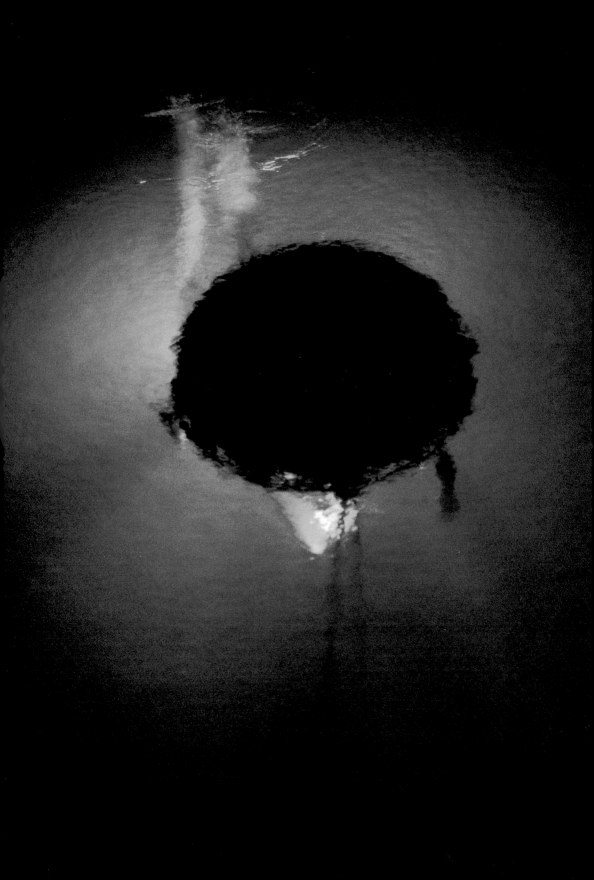

the minimum of effort and preparation, even when working at extreme depths and distances. The 'summit' shots would all, therefore, be his: he would carry the extra-strong pressure-proofed camera that Pete Scoones had designed for this trip on some of the deepest exploratory probes into the spring.

From the moment we arrived in Wakulla Park, Mandy and I were impressed with the amount of equipment Bill had managed to assemble for the expedition. There were two Hascal booster pumps with which we were to mix our own gas concoctions from the truckload of bottled helium, oxygen and nitrogen delivered by Air Products. This array of cylinders stood in serried ranks under the cypress trees. There was a hut crammed full with the very latest high-tech diving toys – underwater cameras, Aqua-Zepp scooters, depth gauges, drysuits, torches, masks of every variety and flippers of every colour; there were lead weights and miles and miles of line. There also was Bill's rebreather, an ordered tangle of cylinders and piping; and strewn out on the beach area at the edge of the spring were the aluminium components that would eventually bolt together to form his famous habitat, as well as the huge lead pods that would anchor it down – all 24,000 lbs of it. Soon its mysteries would be revealed to us.

Everything was a hubbub of activity, with so much still to get ready before the real diving could start. We busied ourselves sorting out the filming equipment, getting to know the rest of the team and finding out more about this fascinating area.

Wakulla seems hardly to have changed for centuries. Stark trees still rise from primeval swamps to provide roosts for hundreds of turkey vultures. Alligators slither down banks when disturbed, and water snakes thread their silent way through the riverside sedges. Egrets and herons stalk frogs in the muddy shallows, placing their long legs delicately just in case any floating log should conceal a submerged row of teeth. The whole area is famous for the richness of its wildlife – indeed it is because Wakulla has long been a nature reserve that indiscriminate diving was always discouraged, although from time to time lucrative arrangements have been struck to let in Hollywood movie-makers. 'The Creature from the Black Lagoon' was filmed at Wakulla, as was 'Airport '77' and some of the early Tarzan films. Terrified 'gators probably kept well out of the way at the sight of Johnny Weismuller wrestling in the water with plastic crocodiles! In theory the alligators enjoy protection, and until recently were considered to be of no

102 The mysterious underwater habitat

particular danger to man. However, earlier in the year an unfortunate swimmer who strayed away from the bowl of the spring was dragged to his death by a twelve-foot adult male. Three 'gators were shot in retaliation, as it was not clear which of them was responsible for the foul deed. You could not help feeling it was a trifle unfair.

Tourists take glass-bottomed boat rides to see the fish and turtles of the clear water spring. Peering into the blue mouth of Wakulla, it is possible to make out the dark hole of the cave entrance under the water. Between seven and thirteen million cubic feet of water pour out of here every day, making it one of the largest springs in the world. It is not clear where all this water comes from. I was hoping we would be able to find a connection with other nearby waterways, for there is something very special about being able to dive into a cave one end and emerge elsewhere. The nearest candidate was a reedy pool called Sally Ward not more than a mile from Wakulla. Some years before a cave had been discovered under the waterweeds which yielded over a thousand feet of drowned passages, going down to a depth of 260 feet. Divers had found a pearly white cavern of monstrous size but so far no link with Wakulla. We decided to make a filming reconnaissance in Sally Ward as part of our acclimatization, and found it so enchanting that we went back there several times.

First came a short swim through tangly weeds, followed by a drop of 30 feet down a narrow shaft, which brought us to a tight constriction choked by hundreds of pieces of waterlogged wood, rounded like pebbles from the continual battering against rocks. We had to wriggle through this maelstrom of floating debris to get to the larger passage beyond. It was a bizarre experience. No sooner did you push your head into this strange swirling tannic mass, than you emerged on the other side into gin-clear water. Film we took down there gives no impression of being underwater at all. It was so startlingly clear that only tell-tale bubbles and the occasional fish give it away.

103 *opposite:* Listening for alligators, Mandy prepares to dive at night into Sally Ward, barely one kilometre from Wakulla
104 *below:* Baby alligators play with mother's tail

Getting through into the main tunnel was a tight squeeze, made no easier by the fact that we were wearing American back-mounted tanks rather than the hip-mounted ones we were used to back home. There is always that moment of claustrophobic panic when you wonder whether, if you fight your way through, you will ever be able to get back out again, but such thoughts are quickly dispelled when you find yourself in a tunnel ten feet high and about the same distance wide. It is as if a gigantic mole had gone in search of adventure into the depths of the earth. The tunnel is more or less symmetrically round, with the exception of odd small rockfalls from the ceiling and slight pockets of weaker rock that have been eroded by the currents. Once inside, you almost have to force yourself to breathe, not due to any physical exertion, but quite simply because the beauty of the colours and the perfection of the cave take your breath away. You cannot believe you are now fifty feet below the surface.

Dozens of black, whiskered catfish hug the pockmarked walls seeking out small items of food that have been washed into the cave. The catfish are not blind, as most cave fish are, but being naturally nocturnal they can cope very well in total darkness. They enter the caves during the day and go outside to feed at night. It is quite frightening to be swimming along and suddenly have one thump into your mask, for they are quite a size. And they swim a long way into the caves. Tom Morris told me of a pair that are found in Devil's Eye, almost a mile back. Every time divers go there, this catfish couple can be seen foraging about. No one has any idea what they find to eat so far from the surface; the only way to learn this would be to kill them and open them up, but who would have the gall to do that?

The strangest creatures in the caves, however, are the blind albino crayfish. These really have adapted to a life of total darkness: their eyes and their colorations have been dispensed with completely over thousands of years of evolution. An old man, who is the crayfish expert of these parts, once collected some cave crayfish to put in an aquarium. That was more than fifty years ago when he was a graduate student at the University of Florida. Those crayfish are still alive! Normal surface crayfish live for only a couple of years at most, whereas these chaps have somehow managed to stretch their lives out, probably in response to a slow lifestyle and the low availability of food. You cannot help wondering whether their secret for longevity is that they have discovered Ponce de León's Fountain of Youth!

105   *above:* Inside Sally Ward the water was so clear you almost forgot to breathe
106   *below:* Caves in Florida are quite different from English ones

11 • MONSTERS OF THE DEEP

It was Gavin who found the tiny alcove and saw, partly buried in its soft white sand, some dark-stained bones that looked as if they had lain there undisturbed for centuries. We had no idea what they might be but, knowing that in the distant past the caves were probably dry, images of sabre-tooth tigers filled our fancy. Or maybe some poor ancient antelope had curled up there to die? We carefully videoed the remains and planned a more thorough investigation later.

That evening, instead of sharing our enthusiasm when we showed him our videotape, Wes Skiles simply roared with laughter.

'I recognize the discs of those bones,' he told us. 'They come from the spine of an alligator.'

Gavin and I felt a bit abashed at this and I quickly dismissed ideas of having a sabre-tooth tiger sketch in the film, but all the same I was intrigued to know how an alligator came to die down there. Somehow, one does not expect an alligator to drown. They can stay underwater for long periods at a time, although of course as reptiles they do need to come to the surface to breathe. I suppose this old fellow swam into the cave in search of food – perhaps following a catfish – only to become disoriented in the pitch darkness. If he could not find the way out, the poor beast would eventually have run out of air and drowned. As Wes sympathetically remarked, this could easily have happened at any time in history. Alligators are among the oldest of animal types, so it is quite possible that the bones we found were as ancient as they looked!

Nevertheless there was good reason why Gavin and I should get so excited about a bunch of old bones. Back in the mid-fifties two students from the University of Florida, the first people to be allowed into Wakulla with scuba equipment, did make a momentous discovery down there. As I had already approached these two pioneers, Garry Salsman and Wally Jenkins, to interview them for the film, I had the privilege of hearing their story first-hand.

107   Garry Salsman and Wally Jenkins today

For some years, Garry, Wally and their friends had been diving the lesser springs in the area, but had consistently been refused access to the 'Big Fella', Wakulla. In 1955 they helped a film crew which was working in the spring, and in return they were at last granted the permission they wanted. With a sense of anticipation, they swam over the great lip at the bottom of the spring basin, and down into the black depths of the cave. On that first dive, narcosis drove them back from about 180 feet, at which point the cave was beginning to level off. The next time they went down, they were able to go a little further towards the section that later became known as the 'Grand Canyon'. Wally had gone ahead to investigate a large piece of limestone that had caught his eye, when suddenly he saw beside it a massive leg-bone, about three and a half feet long. Looking round, he could make out more and more bones, scores of them, scattered all about him.

'I started squeaking like one does under water to call Garry over. There were all these remains of animals that nobody knew about. You can bet we lost interest in limestone formations after that. We were exuberant!'

This discovery was startling enough for the cave owner to let them continue with their exploration after the film people had left for home. In the following months, they went on to find even more remains – and what remains they turned out to be! There were camels, bears, deer, giant sloths, all manner of creatures. Most remarkable of all were the bones later

108   Entering Wakulla in 1955

identified as belonging to the woolly mammoth and to its primitive relative, the mastodon. Such giants had been extinct for thousands of years, but no one seemed sure whether they had coexisted with early man.

Stone-age arrowheads had already been found close to the cave, but in order to prove that Wakulla's large animals and man had roamed these lands together, there would need to be some positive way of linking the relics together. Ideally, Garry and Wally had to find a bone with an arrowhead embedded in it, the bone growing round the arrowhead, if they wanted to prove that the animal had been shot at by a hunter. No amount of searching revealed anything as convincing as that, but they did discover spear points in the same sediment and what looked like traces of charcoal. They also found a midget mastodon, only a quarter of the size of the others but with its teeth worn down, suggesting it was an adult. They found a tusk over seven feet long and very fragile, the ivory having long since been chemically replaced in the fossilization process. For safety's sake, they reburied it and left it down there. Other treasures were brought to the surface. Some of the petrified bones weighed as much as 50 lbs, far too heavy to swim with, so they devised a simple but effective method of lifting them. By inflating a pillowcase lined with a plastic bag, they were able to create just enough lift to raise the enormous fossils out of the cave.

How did these bones of land animals come to be in the flooded cave? Had they merely been washed in by water from somewhere else? It certainly seemed that some sort of grading had taken place – tusks were found in one area, all the rib bones in another, and teeth somewhere else again. Such sorting could well have been the result of current action. Or perhaps, since the majority were found in a single, rubble-filled chamber, they were the remains of creatures who had had the misfortune to fall from the land surface into a concealed cavern through a hole in its roof? Norbert Casteret had found a similar charnel house in the Pyrenees. Garry and Wally found most appealing the theory that the caves may once have been the home of early man, and these dawn hunters the agent that sorted the bones.

Enough bones were found locally for the Museum of Florida History to be able to reconstruct an entire mastodon skeleton. We went to see it and were suitably impressed. In life, a creature like this would have stood higher than nine feet at the shoulder, was longer than sixteen feet, weighed something over ten tons and ate, we were told, some 300 lbs of leafy vegetation every day, just to stay alive! It dated back 12,000 years to a time when Florida was a lot drier than now. With little or nor surface water, springs like Wakulla would have been very important watering holes for all the animals in the area. Perhaps, with the water table being so much lower then, the animals had been forced to negotiate the very steep cave entrance in order to take a drink. The museum palaeontologist felt that this could have accounted for all the large bones down there: many of the bigger animals, unable to climb back up the confined and slippery slope, might have been trapped or trampled to death at the bottom. Whatever happened, it was some slaughter.

In the time between those early explorations and now, there has been a certain amount of looting from the cave. Illicit divers have gone in and come back with mantelpiece trophies, although the mind boggles at the size of mantelpiece required to display a mastodon's tusk or leg-bone. Some scientists were opposed to our expedition, because they felt there should be no further disturbance of such an important site, either from a palaeontological point of view, or in the interest of preserving the delicate deep-cave ecosystem. Just 'because it is there' is no longer justification enough to go dashing in and stirring up the mud of the past, and certainly not for treasure-hunting. This I appreciate. It is always thrilling to go somewhere

few, if any, people have been before, but it must be done cautiously so as to cause the minimum impact. One of the preconditions of our being allowed into Wakulla at all was that nobody should touch or bring out any artefacts from the cave. Only water, rock and mud core samples were taken, along with the odd unfortunate blind crayfish that got swept into divers' nets – and all these were welcomed by the scientific community.

We did find bones. We measured them, we photographed and filmed them. To discover such links with an exotic and long-dead past was very exciting. It gave us an inkling of what it must have been like to be the first people down there, but we kept strictly to the rules and brought nothing back for our mantelpieces.

In their explorations, Garry Salsman and Wally Jenkins pushed beyond the bone bed and the Grand Canyon to a distance of about 950 feet and a depth of 240 feet below the surface. The cave continued, but they had reached the point where a dive involved little more than 'just a mad swim in, turn around, and a mad swim out'; sheer distance ruled out further penetration at that time. In the space of a couple of years, they and their friends had made more than two hundred accident-free sorties in Wakulla, and they had done it with what we would consider the most primitive of equipment. They had a tank of air, a regulator, a facemask so they could see, a pair of fins to push them through the water, and feeble, hand-held torches – that was all. There were no pressure gauges, no buoyancy compensators to control their depth, and all their early dives were made without wetsuits, for although these were on the market they were much too expensive for student pockets. Instead, they wore just a bathing suit with perhaps a sweat shirt over the top. Wally declared it was just possible to stay warm enough during decompression stops so long as they remained perfectly still. That way a layer of water, warmed by their own body heat, would build up around them, and provided nobody swam past and disturbed it they would be just fine. It sounded a little like all those overblown theories proving that the holes in string vests keep you warmer than the string. Give me a suit any time!

Garry showed us a photograph he had taken of Wally underwater – covered in goose-pimples – and told us that it was soon after seeing this picture that Wally was the first to crack. He went out and bought a wetsuit; Garry always suspected he must have had the money stashed away ready. Gradually all the members in their little diving group followed Wally's lead.

109 *above:* Part of their discovery deep inside Wakulla. 'Mastodons, mammoths, deer, bear, you name it . . . '

110 *below:* An inflated pillow-case helps lift a mastodon leg-bone

112   *opposite:* At the start of the Grand Canyon and at a depth of 220 feet. The femur of a mastodon is almost as big as Mandy.

There was a tragic story of how one of their friends left his brand new wetsuit down on the diving jetty when he came in for a cup of coffee. When next he looked it was being attacked by a group of buzzards! They must have thought he was still inside. It was pecked to ribbons and useless after that.

We would have liked to keep these two talking for ever, but finally had to let them go – they were about to set off on a sailing trip in the Gulf of Mexico. Obviously reaching the grand old age of sixty had not meant the end of adventure for either of them.

On the spring bank work was by now well in hand on the construction of Bill's underwater habitat. At last it was possible to visualize how the device was supposed to work. A sophisticated version of the old diving bell, it was a ten-foot diameter hemisphere, like half a giant beachball, which trapped a bubble of air underwater. In this divers would be able to take refuge and perform their decompression routines in some comfort, out of water. They could sit, talk, eat and drink, and maintain contact with the surface by

telephone, so long as they kept breathing the prescribed gas mixtures. The little capsule would be stabilized by an inverted tubular aluminium tripod connected to a deep-level anchor in the bowl of the spring and the whole structure was designed to move up and down in the water like an elevator. In this way, it was planned, the final six decompression stops, the longest, could take place at the required depths in relative luxury.

It was an ingenious idea with more than a whiff of Jules Verne about it, but in theory there seemed no reason why the contrivance should not work. What almost scuppered it − and us − was the way Bill's habitat quickly seemed to develop a life and will of its own, independent of its inventor.

The prefabricated superstructure was assembled with no particular difficulty and lowered by crane into the spring, along with the nine massive lead pods that would be required to anchor it on the awkward slope of the spring basin. This was when we experienced our first setback. As the large lead cylinders were manoeuvred into position on the sloping limestone shelf, two of them rolled over the lip of the basin and were lost in the depths of the cave, leaving nothing but a smoke-trail of silt behind them. At first we thought it would be a relatively simple task to locate and recover them, and we all dived into the water to begin feeling about with our hands in the soft clay directly below where they had fallen.

I, too, joined in this search, after I had shot a little film, and found that the hard exercise of digging through squelchy mud at a depth of over a hundred feet soon brought on the early warning signs of narcosis. Because it was dark down there and I had not had a chance to go into the cave beforehand to familiarize myself with it, I was overcome with a strong feeling of gloom and apprehension. As soon as I stopped digging and went up a matter of ten feet, my head immediately cleared and the gloom washed away.

No one managed to locate either of the pods, and the search was continued with six-foot bamboo rods probing more deeply into the mud. Still the elusive pods remained hidden.

Metal detectors were brought in but these quickly flooded and became useless. Not long afterwards, one of the pods was discovered by a lucky grope in the mud, but it took four days of meticulous searching with the poles and a line grid to find the other. Raising them proved another matter entirely.

Like Wally and Garry with their petrified bones, we were going to have to employ air-filled lift bags, but we were dealing with more than an overgrown elephant's leg here. Each pod weighed 3,000 lbs. Some pretty robust bags would be needed to hoist them up 100 feet. Bill procured some two-ton bags, one of which was attached to the ring in the top of the first pod and air pumped in by the surface compressor. The idea was that the airbag would gently lift the lead back to the surface, but the sucking mud in which they were partly buried forced us to keep pumping in more and more air. When eventually the lead pod was freed from the grasp of the mud, it began accelerating to the surface very rapidly. These airbags have a release valve on top so that surplus air can be spilled to keep them under control, but the amount of air needed to spill quickly if we were to slow down the progress of this runaway contraption was far more than would emerge out of one tiny release valve.

As the lead hurtled upwards like a Saturn moon rocket, clouds of billowing silt following in its wake, everyone scattered in all directions. We did not know what was about to happen, but this instinctive scattering

113 *opposite:* Bill's habitat was decompression chamber, restaurant, photographic studio and transatlantic telephone booth. To alligators it represented the ultimate in fast-food dispensers.
114 *overleaf:* Constructing the habitat underwater

probably saved someone's life. The overfull airbag crashed into the lip of the rock overhang with such force that it burst apart, whereupon the lead, its supporting buoyancy abruptly removed, reversed its impetuous course, and plunged back down towards us in a shower of large rocks. Fortunately none of us was hit, but it was a close shave. The only consolation we could draw was that this time we knew where the pod had landed for it was flagged by the tattered remnants of the exploded airbag.

It was obvious that the same thing would happen again if the lead was not repositioned away from the overhang before trying to raise it. A winch and a block and tackle were summoned to drag the pod up the slope and clear of the lip of the basin. Once in a position to give the airbag a clear run to the top, we all moved back out of the way except for Wes and Paul DeLoach whose job it was to fill the bag with air.

This time there was a new danger we had not foreseen. One of the glass-bottomed boats that bring the tourists for trips around the spring had chosen just the moment of lift-off to circle above us. We gaped horrified as the airbag and lead headed like a guided missile towards it. Wes and Paul both hung on grimly, desperately trying to bleed off the excess air, but to no avail. Once more, the lead was out of control and, realizing there was no force on earth that would stop it shooting to the surface, they peeled off while they still could. Perhaps the boatman saw it coming, for at the very last minute the little glass-bottomed craft steered safely out of the way, just as two tons of lead broke surface and shot clear out of the water!

With the lost weights recovered, we resumed work on the habitat. On the far side of the spring it is relatively shallow and the underwater construction was carried out there, using airbags to raise and lower the various components. Finally, we were ready to put the neoprene-coated, bullet-proof nylon skin over the framework and inflate the whole thing with compressed air. As this was done, it plopped to the surface, but with nowhere near the violence of the lead from the deep! Even so, the habitat had an upward force in the water of something over 16,000 lbs. The ballast cylinders were not managing to anchor it down and the electric winch was unable to lower it.

When the circumference of the dome was measured, we found that the nylon shell – which had been expected to shrink seven per cent in manufacture – had hardly shrunk at all. This meant that the dome was housing more compressed air than it should have been, which accounted for the unexplained extra buoyancy. There was nothing for it but to call for more lead. At first Bill thought 500 lbs would do the trick, but it eventually took four times that amount.

115   Raising the lost pods. When gravity and lead combine they do exactly what they want.

By now, twelve days of our precious six weeks had gone and we were starting to fall behind schedule. However, we were confident that at last everything was ready for the deep dives to begin.

No such luck! When Rob and Gavin went out early next morning they found that the habitat had vanished completely. Peering down into the clear waters of Wakulla failed to reveal its whereabouts. There was nothing for it but to go down and investigate. Quickly getting into diving gear, they found the habitat lodged at a crazy angle, half-full of water at a depth of 90 feet. Many of its electrical components were submerged, although the winch mechanism, luckily, was still clear and dry. They returned to break the news to Bill.

I was able to film the ensuing pow-wow, which had far more immediacy than interviewing people about it afterwards. Everyone was stunned by what had happened. I panned around the circle and the look of disbelief was mirrored from face to face. Like in a silent movie, Bill's mouth opened and shut, but no sound emerged. Why had it happened and how much damage had the habitat and electronic equipment sustained? Would it be possible to get the device back in position, and if so, what was to prevent the same thing happening again?

We began to lose faith in Bill's futuristic vision, which was possibly unfair. There was no way he could have test-run any of this in the laboratory first – these were his sea trials. Suddenly it struck me that had we been inside with the power turned on when the habitat sank, we could all have been electrocuted. It was a sobering thought. Were we right to trust our lives to such an untried contrivance? Maybe the habitat was just a white elephant that belonged in the graveyard with the other relics?

The solution, when we discovered it, was a simple one. The long hose that had been used to fill the capsule with compressed air was not fitted with a non-return valve. When the compressor was switched off during the evening, the air had simply siphoned back out again, sending our precious mobile home to the bottom. Raising it was not so simple, but we achieved it. That left just one more thing. We were all in agreement that the electrical winch had to go: it was far too risky. Precious time was lost while a manual chain hoist was designed and manufactured, but finally everything was operational. Wes said his father used to tell him that anticipation was the greatest thrill in life. By this time we had had about all the anticipation we could stand. It was a good thing we could at last get down to the serious business of deep diving.

116   It is hard to imagine that anything weighing over 16,000 lbs could get lost. Isaac Newton was not always on Bill's side.

12 • MORE PEOPLE HAVE BEEN TO THE MOON . . .

'You can borrow my car, you can borrow my house, you can even borrow my woman . . . but you can't borrow my scooter!'

Sheck Exley's categoric refusal to share his underwater vehicle was the only note of serious disharmony I observed among members during the whole expedition. And it was a reasonable enough denial considering the possible implications: 'If anything goes wrong with my scooter, I die,' Sheck had insisted.

He was simply not prepared to have his life put at risk by anybody else's mishandling of such a vital piece of equipment. It was a sentiment shared by all those lucky enough to own scooters. The fact was that we could have done with several more of these invaluable transporters. A lot of the press coverage we attracted made play of the similarities between our expedition and space exploration. If Bill's high-tech equipment was 'the counterpart of the space ship', as was said, then our Aqua-Zepp DVPs (diver propulsion vehicles) represented a cross between moon-buggy and rocket-pack.

The divers now separated off into teams of two or three for the exploration. Sheck worked, as he usually does, with Paul DeLoach, Wes with Rob Parker and Brad Pecel, and finally there was Paul Heinerth with Tom Morris. Bill himself took little part in this aspect: so much of his time, initially, was spent in bolting, building and testing that when the deep probes started he had not built up the requisite experience with the Aqua-Zepps. Indeed, his first attempt at going into the cave proper ended with him crashing both himself and his scooter into the solid rock walls of what – for the most obvious of reasons – is known as The Restriction. It used to amuse me how somebody like Bill, with his overwhelming command of abstruse theory, would so often be let down by the simple chicanery of life. It was as if in making a cosmic grasp, obvious little everyday practicalities would escape him. He found it hard, for instance, to keep track of his belongings. I remember him saying one morning he could not dive

117   Rob Parker and Wes Skiles prepare for a deep dive into Wakulla

that day because he'd lost his fins; he'd looked everywhere and they were gone. I took the liberty of peeping inside his tent and there, plain to see on top of the mixed salad that was his kit, were the errant flippers! Bill seems to be the eternal optimist, believing always that the amount of energy he puts into one aspect of a problem – even if it leaves him insufficient time to attend to others – will somehow or other balance out and guarantee that all will come right in the end. It did not take me long, though, to realize how wafer thin this optimism was and how easily he was crushed by harsh reality. Setbacks always made Bill retreat inside himself to lick his wounds and reassess the situation. Afterwards he would be back with a modified plan of action.

I have remarked before upon Bill's persistence, and nothing better illustrates this than the way he got into cave diving.

He was a caver, pure and simple, when about fourteen years ago he began exploring a system of caves under the Huautla Plateau in Southern Mexico. The caves ran deep and invariably Bill would come up against underwater sections where a localized fold in the stratum trapped water, much as the U-bend does under a sink. In most cases it was possible with scuba equipment to dive through these loops, or sumps, in order to explore further dry passages beyond, but the deeper into the mountain they went, the deeper were the sumps, and the more it was borne home to Bill that simple scuba was not the answer. There was never any question of him giving up the exploration – he saw the mapping of these caves as one of his missions in life. He wanted to discover an underground spring that could be drilled to provide community water for the impoverished Mazatec Indians who live nearby. Bill considered all possible options in search of a solution.

'I had read of Sheck Exley,' he told me, 'and these other people from Florida who had gone down to Northern Mexico in 1979 and done some really deep diving there. They were doing over 300 feet on air. I thought to myself, "Boy, they must know something. They are all coming out alive!" So I wrote to Sheck and asked him to teach me how to dive. It was getting in through the back door, really.'

The first thing Sheck insisted upon was that he should build up his tolerance by gradually diving to new depths. This was fine by Bill because he reckoned Sheck would always be there to pull him out of any trouble. Their first dive took them down to 140 feet; decompressing on the way out, Bill could not fail to be impressed by the Florida diver.

'There I was, sitting clinging to a log for dear life, trying not to go up or down below the decompression stop, and Exley was just lying there with his hands folded like some pious knight on a tomb, floating there, absolutely horizontal, perfectly stabilized in the water. "My God," I thought, "I've got a lot to learn!"'

They were soon diving to over 200 feet and Bill was feeling pretty good about it. In between dives, he would ply Sheck with questions in order to pick up all the little tricks of the game. Finally, when they were getting ready for their last dive, Sheck pulled out a couple of oxygen bottles.

Oxygen is a good safety measure against the bends on a deep dive, but Bill did not know that, so he was unsure what was happening. They went to a place called Eagle's Nest, deep in savannah north of Tampa, to a pool surrounded by high elephant grass – the kind of place where you expect to find an alligator around every bend. The water there all funnels down a narrow hole; sliding down it was like going down a long, long firemen's pole. At 90 feet it breaks out into a gigantic chamber and the visibility changes from bad to crystal clear, much as it does in Sally Ward. Three of them went down, Bill just behind Sheck and his companion, as they led him wide-eyed along a gigantic tunnel.

'I was really wired! I looked at my depth gauge at about 200 feet and decided not to bother looking at it again, but just concentrate on the dive. I knew I was getting narced.'

The way he described narcosis to me was as a razor-sharp ridge. On the one side you are precariously balanced on rapture – just having a great time, everything going well, euphoric – on the other side, the one you are not aware of, you become affected by delayed psychomotor response. The eye sees, the mind comprehends, but there is a time lapse between command and action. You do not react fast enough. This was what was happening to Bill.

At 240 feet he was figuring, 'Jesus, this is incredible!' but somehow had forgotten to hit his buoyancy compensator as he should have done when heading down this big tunnel. As he turned round to come back, he was still heading downwards and immediately ploughed right into the layer of silt on the floor. He could no longer find the line out of the cave. His only route to salvation had disappeared in zero visibility.

Anxiety caused him to start breathing more rapidly, which immediately increases the narcosis factor, and the carbon dioxide retention.

'All of a sudden you think, "Oh, my God, I am breathing faster! Oh, my God, I can't see the line out of the cave! Oh, Jesus, Jesus!" and this little voice in the back of your head keeps saying, "You are going to die!" and you think, "Oh, sweet Jesus!" and the whole damned cycle starts again!'

As the carbon dioxide builds up, tunnel vision develops.

'The whole thing goes down into this one little hole. I am sitting there stuck in this vicious circle, stuck in the muck on the bottom. But the next thing I see, coming down the long tunnel, is an outstretched hand.'

Sheck had realized in time that Bill was in difficulty.

'Immediately, I grabbed hold of the hand with all my strength – nothing was going to make me let go. Sheck swam me along, pulling me up to 220 feet, and meanwhile the bubbles are crashing like thundering echoes, just reverberating like locomotives through the mind.'

At 220 feet Bill magically came out of his 'tunnel'. The line was in his hand, his head had cleared. All it needed was those 20 feet. It was probably this experience that led him to experiment with mixed-gas diving.

The use of helium in deep diving had got off to a bad start some years before: the first time cave divers used it in the mid-seventies, one man convulsed and died during decompression. That made everyone very wary and several years passed before it was tried again. Then Dale Sweet went

118 *overleaf*: Firing up scooters for a journey into the depths of the earth

down to 360 feet in Diepolder's on it and returned safely. He planted an American flag down there to mark his deepest point, but told no one he had done so. A week later Sheck Exley was able to repeat the dive on air – no helium – and the fact that he reported finding the flag was conclusive proof that he had done so. As soon as everyone heard that Exley had managed to equal the depth on air, there seemed little point in bothering with potentially lethal helium. A couple of years later John Zumrick had come to a much better understanding of the science involved and had produced far more accurate decompression tables; the German cave diver Jochen Hasenmeyer had been down as far as 476 feet safely on helium. This made everyone sit up and take notice, and Bill Stone began his mixed-gas diving experiments that led in turn to our Wookey dive, and on to Wakulla.

Sheck Exley is a school teacher. At thirty-eight, he is generally acknow-ledged as one of the world's most experienced cave divers. He is the man who has pushed hardest and furthest; he has written the standard work on the subject, and has done more to develop Floridan diving than anyone. To his sport, he is what Reinhold Messner is to mountaineering. Having been on expeditions with each of them, I find it uncanny to see in how many ways these two resemble each other. Like Messner in his prime, Exley really prefers to be alone on his extreme exploits. He feels no need for a companion, when to have one only doubles the likelihood of things going wrong. This was something bitter experience had taught him. In Africa once, he was diving 3,000 feet horizontally underwater with a companion whose two diving systems chose to malfunction simultaneously. If they were going to get out at all, it was plain they would have to do it by buddy-breathing. Sheck's partner became so agitated that he was drawing three breaths to every one of Sheck's. At that rate they would run out of air long before getting back to their first staged cylinder. Indeed, the pressure gauge was already reading almost empty and it was becoming increasingly difficult to pull out the last breaths of air. They had to swim the final 50 feet without air at all. Gasping and spluttering for breath, they both drew on the first cylinder and continued outward.

When the same thing started to happen again – and again due to Sheck's companion over-breathing – Sheck coolly checked his friend's contents gauge and ascertained there were just enough atmospheres left to get him to the next staged cylinder. That way they made it back to the daylight. If Sheck had panicked in any way, or altered his own breathing rate, they would surely both have been down to their last breath and died.

I was curious to know how he felt and asked him whether for a moment he had considered hanging on to his own air to be sure of getting out himself? His reply cut me short.

'You don't think like that, do you?'

I still wanted to know how he faced the prospect of dying, dying for what would have been the want of only a few breaths had they not reached those two staged cylinders in time? He simply said, 'All I could think about was how sad it would be to die in this cave in Africa with nobody knowing why.'

When he was only fourteen years old, Exley had seen his brother drown in this very spring at Wakulla. It was one of those accidents that should never have happened. Thinking that they might be able to free-dive down from the cave rim to the floor at 100 feet, his brother had hyperventilated his lungs by breathing deeply, then gone over the edge. Tragically, he blacked out and sank to the bottom. Seconds later he resurfaced unconscious, only to disappear again. Sheck rushed to get a cylinder of air and a regulator, but by the time he managed to retrieve his brother, he was deeply unconscious and remained so until that night, when he died.

As he approaches forty, Sheck realizes that he has only a few more years left to operate at extreme level. The older you are, the more prone you become to the bends, and mental alertness is not so acute as it was. Above all, the physical effort required is difficult for someone in middle age to sustain. Not enough is understood about the long-term effects of diving, but prolonged activity is known to cause bone deterioration. Before it became too late for him Sheck wanted to hold the cave diving depth and distance records. (Some time after Wakulla he did just that, going over 10,400 feet horizontally in Chip's Spring, near Tallahassee in Florida – the world's longest cave dive – and reaching a stunning depth of 780 feet in Nacimiento in Mexico.)

Though in practice roles would blur, Sheck was obviously our main hope for pushing deep into Wakulla. It was Wes's task to bring back film of new territory, and the other pair were to conduct scientific investigations. When you consider his caution about letting anyone tamper with his scooter, it is ironic that Sheck's vehicle almost brought our expedition to a disastrous end. Exploring what we called D Tunnel, which was found to penetrate 3,600 feet and 300 feet deep, Sheck's Aqua-Zepp failed and, being towed by Paul DeLoach's scooter, he was just able to make it back to the habitat using the emergency supply depots of air.

Wes Skiles, a native of Florida, is a chubby extrovert, always ready with a smart answer or a fascinating story. His good humour made him the butt of much teasing. Brad, his partner, is tall, blond and silent, his perfect foil in

almost every way. Though he chooses now to live in the Bahamas, Brad comes from California, where his good looks could easily have made him into a movie star. One day, we had all been fantasizing about Bo Derek (as one does on expeditions!), when Noel Sloan, our physiologist, remarked, 'If you rate her as 10 on a scale from 1 to 10, what would be the male equivalent? How would we all rate?'

Brad would have to be 10 – we all agreed on this.

'And me?' questioned Wes.

Noel cast a telling glance in his direction and said, 'Well . . . 1!'

'I would have thought I'd have made it to at least 2,' Wes pleaded piteously. After that, whenever 10 or 2 were mentioned on the expedition, we all dissolved into laughter.

Most of Wes's diving had been in local springs and he has logged over 3,000 cave dive 'penetrations'; he knows more about Florida's 'aquifer' than perhaps anyone, and works now as an environmental consultant. After years of being considered crazy for his blind devotion to the sport, the novelty of enjoying recognition for all his experience gives him a good deal of pleasure. He is dedicated to preventing the contamination of Florida's vast freshwater reserves by incautious development.

In Wakulla, we had identified three side tunnels off the main one, all of which we wanted to take a good look at. With so much exploratory work to be done, Wes announced that he could afford to dedicate only two deep dives to pure filming. We were alarmed, therefore, when we got rushes back from his first trip to find all the film was out of focus. There was obviously some camera fault and I had a nasty suspicion that Wes's second batch of film would be similarly affected. If so, I could not imagine how we were going to break the news to him; he had worked so hard at getting what we wanted. We would somehow have to persuade him to go down and have another shot at it.

It was important for me to take some footage inside Bill's habitat to show viewers what it was like and how it worked. I went down one evening to meet Wes and the rest of his team decompressing in there after one of their long dives. This refuge was proving to be a real home from home. I can see nobody will ever want to go deep diving without one in future. The worst part of decompression is when you are immediately below it, when you can see the habitat tantalizingly close, but may not yet go inside. It is hard to imagine how people can bear the non-activity of decompressing in water, time and time again. For just a few minutes of productive exploration, you

119 *above:* Filming in B Tunnel over half a mile from the surface
120 *below:* Each had to carry over 1,200 cubic feet of synthetic gases for such a journey

pay with so many hours of hanging about. What do you find to think about in all that time? You can read a book, but the pages get soggy. It is not unusual for a paperback to be divided among the divers at any given depth-stage, and then left there afterwards for the next ones who pass that way. How terrible to get to the end of a whodunit and find the critical page has floated away!

Wes had suffered from bends in the past, so he takes longer than most at all the decompression stops. Eventually, however, we were sitting comfortably in the capsule, convivially swapping jokes and stories. Mandy had sent us down a roast chicken, which for all I know was the first meal of its kind ever to be eaten underwater, and Wes was in fine form. As always, he had the best shaggy dog story to match the occasion.

'These guys were out on a ranch,' it began, 'and so they had to cook, which none of them enjoyed. They worked out a system whereby whoever complained about the food became the cook. One day a new hand came in, ate some of the food and said, "Man, this is really shitty stuff!" He couldn't understand why everybody was laughing until they explained how he had landed the job of cooking for all of them. Well, this poor guy cooked and he cooked and he cooked − weeks on end he cooked − and nobody complained about the food. So he decided to fix it once and for all. He went out and found the biggest old moose turd he could find and baked that into a pie.

'That night, he put the pie out there and − you know it − the biggest, meanest cowboy of all came by, Black Bart. Black hollered, "Give us a slice of that pie, boy!" He took a bite out of the pie, and spat it straight back on to his plate. "Urgghh!" he roared, "moose turd pie!" Then, remembering the rules, he added with an evil smile, "But it's good!"'

It was while we were all chuckling that Mandy rang through from the surface to say that the second film Wes had taken was also spoiled. Peter Scoones had modified the camera to go down to 1,000 feet, and he had tried to foresee all the things that could possibly go wrong at great depths, but in the end it proved to be a common-or-garden fault that had blurred the film. The lens had worked loose in its mounting and was no longer able to focus correctly. Listening to my end of the conversation, Wes picked up the gist of it. Since there was no way now of choosing the right moment to tell him, I handed the phone across and let him speak to Mandy direct.

My video camera was still rolling, and I turned it upon Wes as he learned the awful truth. His face betrayed all the emotions of loss. I was surprised how badly he was taking it, until I learned that a couple of weeks earlier he had been inside a cave getting some complicated filming shots when exactly the same thing had happened. 'It's the story of my life,' he muttered gloomily, and turned his face to the wall.

For a long while he was uncharacteristically quiet, bemoaning only that nobody knew the effort that went into shooting film at those depths. 'It sure doesn't come easy!' But his sulk did not last long, and afterwards he volunteered to try again.

On his third attempt he overloaded himself by putting a second Video-8 underwater camera high on a pole behind his scooter to give an over-the-shoulder effect. During the dive Wes lost a lead block from beneath his scooter, this so altered his trim and buoyancy that he kept tipping upside down and it was as much as he could do to get back out of the cave safely. On his fourth and last try he came back with some marvellous footage, showing caverns where no man and no light had ever been before. He once remarked to me that more men had been on the moon than had been inside Wakulla Springs. Certainly those beamed-back pictures from the moon were no more hard-won than Wes's from the deep.

During the last days of the expedition, before work began on dismantling the habitat, Wes, with Tom Morris and Paul Heinerth, mounted one last trip to the furthermost reaches of the cave. It was an 80-minute race against time into B Tunnel that took them 4,500 feet from the cave entrance and 310 feet deep! They laid an additional 1,580 feet of line beyond that which the

121   *below:* After a dive of over 80 minutes at a depth of 300 feet the divers return to the
       habitat to decompress, eat, and relate their adventures
122   *overleaf:* Oxygen helped the divers to flush out nitrogen from their blood. Being
       interviewed for English TV audiences helped to relieve the boredom.

expedition had already laid. The tunnel continued. As Bill Stone later described it, 'They did one *hellacious*, off-the-edge dive. When you get that far and that deep and see how fast your pressure gauges go down, it makes you want to get religion or hang up your scuba tanks for good. With every breath, your pressure goes down.'

Wes had taken the precaution of filling up three line reels before they set off. It is hard to imagine exactly what was going through their minds in deciding to take this last push. They went so far from the entrance and so near to the limits of their air supplies that they were lucky to make it out alive. Tom Morris *did* run out of air but thankfully there were staged cylinders still unused. A scooter failure would almost certainly have finished one of them off. They turned back only when Wes had laid his last inch of line, and then they bolted for home. Even so, Wes managed to make a map on the way out; he firmly believes that surveying is a vital part of diving. You owe it, he insists, to future teams.

Altogether, over a two-month period, we had made 300 man-dives. Besides the long dive in B, we penetrated the Main Tunnel to a length of 3,300 feet, C to 2,900 feet and reached the end of D at 3,600 feet. In all four we went down to around 300 feet. A dye-trace proved that Wakulla is linked to Indian Springs, which is one and a half miles away as the crow flies, but we do not yet have the capability to take us that far underwater.

The next step, Wes told me, is 'saturation cave diving'. He explained this as being able to go in and out of a habitat that is constructed way inside one of these massive, deep conduit systems like Wakulla.

'The habitat would be your base camp and you would live in it for up to two months, exploring from it. You wouldn't go back to the surface, and that way you could get a really long way and wouldn't have to decompress until you finally did re-emerge. Your gases would be replenished by teams working from the surface. One or two decompression dives over a month has to be a lot better for you than a decompression dive every other day as we are doing at present.'

I asked him when he foresaw all this happening.

'Ten years,' he predicted confidently, adding, 'You know, I live here and this is my playground. I have plenty of time. I realize I'm going to get older and it is going to be harder for me to do the things I can do now, but I will just have to change that with technology!'

123 On the last day of the expedition Bill spent 24 hours underwater using his rebreather. During the process he read three novels. Luckily for his experiment the 'gators stayed away.

Wes is twenty-nine, so time should be on his side. He is married and has a young son, but he has never for a moment considered giving up cave diving.

'It is incredibly important to my sanity,' he explains. 'I get a fix down there. That pushing out, exploring and mapping, the sensation of going places that no human has ever been before gives me a satisfaction I can't describe to anyone.'

So long as he devotes himself totally to what he is doing, he knows he is being as responsible as he can to his family and to all the other people who rely on him.

'There is never a thought about the surface while I am underwater, never a single flicker of the fact that the surface even exists. It's your choice, you know. Would you want to be thinking about other things than what you are doing right there, when what you are doing is considered to be one of the riskiest sports on earth? All I want to think about is how to stay alive and maximize the enjoyment.'

His dream then, and Bill's exploration dream are bound together, though they may have come about by different routes.

Bill has every reason to feel proud of his Wakulla expedition. There is little more we could have hoped for: his habitat had proved itself sound and taught us we could live safely underwater; and on the last day of the expedition proper, he tested his rebreathing unit successfully on a single continuous dive of twenty-four hours' duration. His original intention had been to spend all that time in the water, but after twelve hours his drysuit sprang a leak and he began to feel the cold. The solution was nearby. He quickly went into the habitat, dragging his rebreather after him, and spent the next eight hours in relative warmth, but still breathing from his apparatus. Then finally, for the last four hours, he returned to the water and swam around the shallows contemplating the garfish and mullet. Luckily for him, the alligators kept a discreet distance.

It was a strange sight, seeing Bill swimming there with what looked like a loaded kitchen-table on his back and no bubbles coming from his facemask. The contraption weighed a hefty 192 lbs, but he already knows how this can be made more compact. His next model will be infinitely lighter. What is important is that his faith in the technology had been vindicated. He always said he did not want his epitaph to read, 'He screwed up.' And he did not screw up.

Those of us who know him no longer consider that his aim of walking in space is mere fantasy. I, for one, have decided that if Bill is going to the moon, I should like to go with him.

Appendix:
NOTES ON PHOTOGRAPHY

Technology is constantly changing and the choice available to the adventure photographer is rapidly expanding – though there is always the danger of having too much equipment and of being unable quickly to access the appropriate lens in a given situation.

Canon cameras are usually my first choice for stills photographs, and I use T90 and T70 bodies with a range of lenses. The new array of zoom lenses does tend to reduce the number of separate items to be carried and I find the 35–105mm about as versatile as one could wish. With a second zoom in the 100–300mm range and a wide-angle lens of around 24mm one can cover almost any eventuality. Built-in motor winds are the norm and autofocus lenses have almost eliminated out-of-focus shots these days, but with any of the present thirty methods of exposure metering it is still quite possible to be fooled when it comes to getting the right f. stop. As one cameraman put it recently, 'Unless you have grey racing cars against grey backgrounds and grey skies then you might as well forget any of these through-the-lens methods.' This may be an exaggeration but it is as well to understand the limitations of modern equipment.

Adventure movies, to my mind, are best shot on 16mm film, although I can see that with the advent of high definition video 'chip' cameras and Beta SP we will see a gradual changeover in the next few years. An Aaton 16mm has remained my preference as the mainstay camera, with smaller Photosonics for point-of-view shots, and of course for skydiving. Canon have come up with a superb zoom lens ranging from an amazing 7–56mm which is ideal for restricted work, such as in balloon baskets, even though the telephoto end remains rather short.

BALLOONING OVER THE HIMALAYAS

In all balloon flights you are limited to what you can fasten to the balloon. A plywood box was suspended from the widest point of the balloon and aimed at our basket. Inside were two cine cameras: a Photosonic IVN with 100-watt heater, and an Elmer Perkins N9 as back-up. The stills camera was a Canon T70 with 20mm lens. This I trusted to 'Automatic Exposure' and was not disappointed. I had no choice really, for it was dark when we took off, and enjoyed high-altitude brightness within an hour. Besides my Aaton 16mm camera in the basket, I fixed a further T70 with a Canon 14mm ultra wide-angle lens. To cover the take-off and foreground shots, Mandy had two Canon T70s with 35–105mm and 70–210mm zooms. Film was Kodachrome 64.

PARACHUTING AND SKYDIVING

In recent years the professional skydiving cameraman would wear on his helmet a video as well as a stills camera. To this I add my Photosonic 16mm camera for better quality moving pictures and for slow motion. Norman Kent would add a Hasselblad camera, bringing the all-up weight to almost 30 lbs! To give my three formats the same image size, I use a 35mm with a Canon T90, a 10mm for film and an 8mm for video.

In the picture opposite the Contents page you can see the system working on 'The Camera Helmet' which I have designed and marketed for adventure sports activities. To counteract the hard shock of opening the parachute, I have invented a self-contained parachute within the helmet. Should the helmet fall off for any reason, it will float down safely to earth. I have tested it and I assure you it works. I have also devised pressure switches to trigger the cameras. I use two linked together by a T-piece from which a short tube enters my mouth. If I suck once the relay locks on the cine camera; if I suck again it switches off. When I blow, as down a straw into a milk shake, the stills camera is triggered, thus leaving both my hands free for the skydive. Unless your mouth forms a seal around the tube it will not operate. This avoids wasting film and pictures in a noisy aeroplane where you might not otherwise hear the shutter operating.

ON THE EIGER

Having once said that the only way to hold a camera in freefall was on a helmet, I subsequently found that there was a case for hand holding for movies. The only way I could rotate my camera around fast enough to follow Apples as we fell down the Eiger North Face was to hold it in my left hand. My right hand was kept free to open the parachute. In this case the last thing I was trying to do was to film a smooth controlled fall. When we jumped it was −25°C, and to this was added a wind chill factor of about 160 mph. It was not surprising that on one jump the camera froze solid. As we fell through a temperature inversion, the humidity froze forming nearly a centimetre of ice around the camera and my hand!

WITH WHILLANS IN THE ANDES

The weird mushrooms that form in Patagonia are a photographer's dream. Early morning or late evening gave the snow a texture and the mountains relief. A selection of lenses, ranging from 1200mm to fisheye, is necessary to do justice to this subject. On the mountain, the minimum requirement was a short zoom lens of 35–105mm.

CAVE DIVING PHOTOGRAPHY

A few years ago I would have said that skydiving photography was about as difficult as it comes. I was wrong. Cave diving in totally black underwater passageways is infinitely harder to do well, and the techniques are quite different from those one would use above ground. The darkness is the first obvious problem, but simply surviving also requires a certain concentration. Salt water in particular is a hazard to cameras, as Peter Scoones discovered one day when his Arriflex flooded. He quickly surfaced, washed the camera in fresh water and stripped it down. He caught it just in time before corrosion set in.

In dark caves you need to be able to feel the controls and guess the focus. When filming I would use fix-focus lenses on the Photosonic or N9 with either a 5.7mm or 3.5mm fisheye. Refraction underwater increases the focal length, so the wide-angle effect is slightly lost. Pete had a sophisticated housing for his Arriflex, complete with 9–50mm zoom. The fact that he could focus and zoom underwater was a tremendous help, but the bulky housing made him less versatile in English caves. In the Bahamas and Wakulla, where the passageways are bigger, it had no disadvantage. For deep filming he housed a second Arri in an extra-strong tube that would go, he said, to over 1,000 feet.

Filming was only made possible by taking down as many as four 250-watt lamps, each lasting for about half an hour. With these lights you could at least see your subject, but stills pictures seemed even harder goals. You need flash and slave flashes, which often fail to function, and it becomes difficult to judge if two or more flash units have been triggered simultaneously. Most triggering devices rely upon infra-red beams which are readily absorbed underwater.

IN WAKULLA CAVES, FLORIDA

There are always arguments, when filming in caves, about whether to mount cameras in watertight housings or to use Nikons which are said to be waterproof anyway. Whichever are chosen, it is better to avoid reflex viewing because composition in the viewfinder is less exact and seeing the depth of field becomes impossible.

Second only to the air supply in importance in Wakulla was the PAG computerized battery charger. This box of electronic tricks would charge a 7-amp-hour 24-volt battery in about three hours, instead of the normal twenty-four. As we would flatten four film lights every day, it was invaluable and was run almost constantly for six weeks.

POSTSCRIPT

After our return from the Eiger, when Eric had made his solo ascent, someone broke into my car, which I had left parked in a London street. The car was so loaded-up that it was difficult to see at a glance what exactly had been lifted out through the broken side window. Two of my stills cameras appeared to have gone, but fortunately the cine cameras had been tucked away and so were not stolen. Some while later, after driving home, I received a phone call late at night from a woman who claimed her small son had found a box of film cans in the muddy Thames bank at Deptford. They contained all the undeveloped slides of Eric's solo climb. The Thames is tidal at Deptford and salt water could have washed away the emulsion. I phoned my friend Peter Cole at ITN and he immediately arranged to collect the slides by despatch rider, have them washed and developed. Fortunately the pictures were saved – young Tony Pitman received a new fishing rod for his rescue.

ACKNOWLEDGMENTS

As in my earlier book, *Filming the Impossible*, I should like to thank Audrey Salkeld for rendering my diaries, notes and rough drafts into the form of a readable book; Tony Colwell, our adventurous editor at Jonathan Cape; and Adrienne Gear for her sympathetic design.

To all those who helped to prove that *anything* really *is* possible, I would like to extend a specially warm note of appreciation – to balloonists Chris Dewhirst and Brian Smith, Per Lindstrand and Richard Branson; to skydivers Pete Reynolds, Norman Kent, Sharkey, Paul Applegate, Charlie Shea-Simmonds, Darcy, and the Royal Marines among many others; climbers Ron Fawcett, Brian Molyneux, Chris Noonan, Dave Cuthbertson, Hannes Stälhi, Heinrich Harrer, Anderl and Trudi Heckmair, and Eric Jones; to cave divers Graham Balcombe, Garry Salsman, Wally Jenkins, Martyn Farr, Sarah Cunliffe, Rob Palmer, Ian Rolland, Julian Walker, Gavin Newman, Dr Bill Stone, Wes Skiles, Pete Scoones and Rob Parker.

I must also acknowledge help from journalists Peter Gillman and Peter Mason, and from Ian Phillips for electronic gubbins. I owe much else besides to my sky-diving partner Mandy, who doubles as my wife.

PICTURE CREDITS

For those pictures in the book that are not my own, thanks are due to – Mandy Dickinson: 3, 4, 6, 7, 12, 26, 82, 83, 84; *Daily Telegraph* Picture Library: 30; Peter Macpherson: 33, 56; Simon Ward: 36; Ludwig Gramminger: 53; Rick Sylvester: 70, 71; Gavin Newman: 75, 76, 77, 80, 104, 105, 106, 112; Rob Palmer: 81, 85, 86, 87, 88; Rob Parker: 90; Bill Stone: 92, 93, 97, 98; Garry Salsman and Wally Jenkins: 101, 108, 109, 110, 111; and Audrey Salkeld's archives.